Mark,

your father
and wisdom
a source of insp[...]
encouragement to me!

Thank you for your friendship
and for endorsing my book!

Bill Burkhardt

Discovering God Enjoys You

# DISCOVERING
# GOD
## *Enjoys*
# YOU

## A Pathway to Finding
## Your True Identity

BILL BURKHARDT

XULON PRESS

Xulon Press
2301 Lucien Way #415
Maitland, FL 32751
407.339.4217
www.xulonpress.com

Paperback ISBN-13: 978-1-6628-5232-9
Ebook ISBN-13: 978-1-6628-5233-6

"*Discovering God Enjoys You* is not only a deep look into God's heart for people, especially the saints of God, it is also a look into Bill's heart. I have known Bill for many years, and I can say that he has a heart for God and people like few others I know.

It has been my privilege to watch Bill's relationship with our Heavenly Father grow and grow in increasing joy. Bill is uniquely qualified to write about discovering how God enjoys you because of his journey and the many who have been richly blessed through Bill's prophetic and teaching ministry.

Every page is in-depth insight into God's love and acceptance for His children. Immediately, Bill lays the foundation for a marvelous embrace of how much Father God loves and enjoys you. The insights lay a foundation for every other relationship one might have. Bill establishes this truth through the scriptures and many illustrations taken from his experience. He also illustrates the experience of others to whom he has ministered over many years.

I am sure you will enjoy reading *Discovering God Enjoys You* and believe you will reread it several times. You will also want to recommend it to your friends."

**Dr. George Runyan**
Lead Pastor of City Church Ministries, San Diego, CA

"It is my privilege to recommend to you Bill Burkhardt's new book, *Discovering God Enjoys You*. This book draws upon the decades-long experience of a pastor and Kingdom leader in the body of Christ. Bill has heard the cry of those he has led in their search for the revelation of the heart of the Father toward them. In this book, Bill opens a door to understanding how we actually bring pleasure and joy to the Father! Your thinking will be shifted, and you will walk with renewed confidence and joy in Him once again after you finish reading."

**Dr. Mike Hutchings**
Director of Education, Global Awakening, President, God
Heals PTSD Foundation

"Pastor Bill Burkhardt's passion for teaching identity is unique, powerful, and infectious. The revelation that God not only loves us, but actually *enjoys us* is Holy Spirit anointed. Bill shares numerous examples of God pursuing man, and Pastor Bill states, 'that God wants each one of us to make a free-will choice to love Him! We are the object of His joy.' Do yourself a favor...read this book and get Pastor Bill in front of your group. You will be blessed, and so will they!"

**Larry Peltier M.Div.**
Senior Pastor, Open Heavens Church

"*Discovering God Enjoys You* is pleasantly laced with analogies and examples that paint word pictures which make our Father's love and His enjoyment of you burst alive. Expect some satisfying 'ah-ha' moments.

Bill has been a dear friend for ten years, and much of our time together has been in his home, over coffee or on mountain hikes. Bill is a deep well of godly character and rich insights into the heart of God. I can say, without reservation, that Bill embodies the subject that he's presenting. He loves talking about our Father's love and enjoyment for us and will happily 'turn aside' to make sure you feel loved and valued.

You're going to feel warmly enjoyed by a Heavenly Father who is about to become more real, more near and more dear than you every knew was possible."

**Mark Hendrickson**
Author of *Supernatural Provision*

# CONTENTS

# ACKNOWLEDGMENTS

A special thanks to my wife for walking this adventure with me. Your belief in me and that this teaching was vitally needed has encouraged me to write and release this transformational truth to bring others into discovering God's enjoyment of them. I want to acknowledge the late Dr. Graham Truscott and Pamela Truscott for the foundational truths and training I received from them in my early years in Christ. Thank you to everyone whose optimism and faith inspired me to write. Thank you, Krista Dunk, for your expertise as my editor. Thank you to Xulon Press for making my first book publishing experience a joy.

# INTRODUCTION

As a health inspector, a life-transforming experience happened one afternoon when I visited a small Mexican restaurant. After introducing myself, I walked into the kitchen and noticed about six employees involved in food preparation. There was Hispanic style music playing in the background, and in the dining room there were a handful of customers, eating. There was a tangible atmosphere of interpersonal warmth as I observed the employees interact. This restaurant was a business, but it felt like a healthy family.

Even though I didn't understand the lyrics of the Hispanic music, it was likely some form of worship because I could feel the Lord's presence. My attention was drawn to an older Mexican woman preparing food. She was quietly and contentedly preparing food, and she was not paying attention to me. It felt like she was the "grandmother" of that restaurant family.

As I was looking at her, I felt a surge of the Lord's joy for her. The Lord was revealing to me her priceless value. The Lord showed me she was both the culinary and the spiritual matriarch of this restaurant family. The atmosphere in the restaurant was an expression of her heart. She had a gift of hospitality, a gift for preparing good food and the heart of a spiritual mother. The Lord showed me she had been faithful for years to consistently love and pray for the employees in her restaurant.

I was excited about what the Lord was showing me, so I approached one of the younger employees. Asking her if she was bilingual, I explained to her I had a word of encouragement for the older woman in the kitchen. The younger woman said the older woman would need my words translated to Spanish, but none of the employees in the restaurant were proficient enough to translate for me. I asked her, "Would it be okay for me to encourage the older woman if I found someone to translate?" She said yes.

I went out to the dining room and saw a man sitting by himself, eating a late lunch. I asked him if he was bilingual, and he said yes. I explained to him I was a pastor and a health inspector, and had a prophetic word for a lady in the kitchen. "Would you be willing to translate?" To my surprise, he told me he was familiar with the gift of prophecy and he would love to translate for me. So, we walked into the kitchen. The entire group of employees gathered around us. And I began to give her the prophetic word as everyone listened.

While I was prophesying, after a few moments, I noticed several of the younger employees were crying, and then most of them began to cry. We were all experiencing God's love and His tangible presence. I continued with my prophetic word for several more minutes, and then asked them what was happening.

One by one, they began to speak to me through the translator. They all told me my words to this woman were amazingly accurate. They knew they must be experiencing a miracle because I didn't know this woman. They told me she was incredibly kind and loving, and her kindness and prayer had been life changing for many of them. Though most were not blood relatives, they confirmed that everyone working in the restaurant interacted like family.

At this point, we all began to recognize and be grateful for God's goodness. One of the younger employees asked me to pray for them. One by one, I prayed and prophesied over everyone in the group.

The tangible presence of God continued to increase as we felt His pleasure for how we were loving one another. This was a cross-cultural miracle!

I noticed several of the younger employees talking on their phones. They were calling some of their family and friends to tell them a miracle was happening in the restaurant. They were saying, "The health inspector is a man of God, and we are experiencing the love of God through his words." They told them, "Please come to our restaurant now if you want to be part of this."

The series of prophetic words continued for about 30 minutes. It was about 3:30 p.m., and remarkably, no new customers entered the restaurant. There was still Hispanic worship music playing in the background. The Lord supernaturally and sovereignly turned a restaurant into a church for about an hour!

I thanked the translator for being willing to interrupt his lunch for me, and he invited me to join him at his table. He finished his lunch as celebrated what we had just experienced. God prompted me to begin to discuss the story of Joseph in the book of Genesis. I told him we sometimes need God to help us forgive people who have hurt us. God helped Joseph forgive his brothers, and because of his forgiveness, Joseph was blessed and promoted. Then, I started to get a prophetic word for this man. Our eyes met, and I told him, "God wants to unlock anything that might be blocking the financial blessing of your business. God really wants you to be blessed financially."

This man then told me his story. He said he was a building contractor, and his business had been struggling financially because clients had refused to pay him for construction work he had completed. He told me he had been a member of a local church about eight years prior. The pastor asked him to be the lead contractor for the construction of a new church building. After completing the new church building, the church owed him a large amount of money. When he asked the pastor to pay him what he was owed, the pastor refused. So, he was hurt and bitter toward the church for this financial injustice, and he had not attended any church since then.

While he was telling me his story, I knew God wanted to help him forgive the pastor and others who had not paid him. I told him God intends to bless him financially, and He wants to remove his bitterness toward this pastor that was partially blocking the flow of his financial blessing. Assuring him God did not condone the financial injustice, I explained how God wanted to help him to fully forgive. He agreed, and sitting at the restaurant table, I led him in a prayer of forgiveness for those who didn't pay him for his work. Then, I felt a surge of faith to pray for his business to be blessed financially.

The Lord was moved by this man's willingness to translate my prophetic words for the restaurant staff, and so He wanted enable this man's forgiveness so the blockages to his financial blessing could be removed. God had turned a humble, family-owned Mexican restaurant into a dramatic expression of heaven's comfort, encouragement and freedom!

As you can see, God is in the business of transforming people with His love. The biggest breakthrough of my spiritual life happened when God helped me experience His joy for me, and I wrote this book because I want you to understand how much He enjoys you. If you can understand and experience God's joy for you, it will transform your identity and bring new levels of joy and freedom to your life.

In this book, I will be sharing insights and principles from the Bible along with more supernatural stories of how God partnered with me to help people discover how much God values and enjoys them. I invite you to take a journey with me to discover just how much God enjoys you.

# CHAPTER 1

# God Created You Because He Enjoys You

How pleasant it is when we discover someone enjoys us! We love to see a sparkle in someone's eye who is very dear to us, knowing we bring them delight. Our heart gets filled with strength when we know we are accepted and enjoyed. We read in both the Old and New Testament the clear message of joy from God. "Do not sorrow, *for the joy of the LORD is your strength*" (Nehemiah 8:10). Jesus Himself reiterated the Father's message for us in John 15:11, "I have told you this so that *my joy may be in you and that your joy may be complete.*"

The greatest infusion of strength a person can experience is the strength that comes from being *enjoyed by God.* God designed us to be enjoyed. In fact, humans were created because God could not contain His joy (Proverbs 8:30-31), and wanted a family to share in His bliss. This expansion of joy can be seen when a married couple starts a family. As the couple's expresses joy for one another, they conceive a child, who then becomes the object of their parents' enjoyment. Just like a newborn infant brings great joy and delight to their parents, the Godhead created people as the object of His enjoyment.

Joy was the also the Lord's motive for redeeming people (Psalm 19:5, Matthew 13:44, Luke 15). Why does Jesus so passionately pursue people so He can rescue and redeem them? It is because God is not willing to live without the joy of being with us. The Gospel is good news from man's perspective because we can enjoy a fully restored relationship with God based on what Christ has done. But the Gospel is good news from God's perspective He removes every barrier so He can enjoy His kids. That is why joy was the main theme when the angel announced the birth of Jesus. The angel said, *"Behold, I bring you good tidings of great joy which will be to all people"* (Luke 2:20). The angel knew Jesus would bring joy to the world as the world discovered that God enjoys them.

Scripture tells us that the Lord's joy is our strength (Nehemiah 8:10). Our capacity to believe the Lord enjoys us is absolutely vital for our spiritual strength. But believing this truth is not enough. We must learn to receive the Lord's joy. As we allow God to enjoy us, His joy is an energy source for our hearts. Your heart is like a solar panel; it is designed to receive the power and warmth of God's joy and convert it into energy.

Negative experiences with people can block your ability to receive love from God. Even from our infancy, our understanding of our value is based on how people treat us. People, including our parents, are rarely able to interact with us in a way that accurately demonstrates our true value to God.

If you have developed an entrenched view of your own inferior identity, you will have trouble believing the Lord delights in you. But the Lord is determined to help you fully discover the joy He has for you; joy which will restore you back to a correct understanding of your true value.

Imagine you are a woman, recently engaged to a man. Picture yourself entering a room full of unfamiliar people, all preoccupied in conversation. You are looking for your fiancé in the crowd, but you can't find him. Suddenly, he notices you. As your eyes meet from across the room, you see a wave of delight come over his face. His face begins to light up, and he can't take his eyes off you. His radiant face shines so brightly that it warms you right down to your heart. Even though you've had a hard day, your exhaustion melts away as you feel invigorated by your fiancé's joy for you.

This is how the Lord enjoys you! Jesus calls Himself "the Bridegroom" (Mark 2:19). Your Bridegroom has designed you to be filled with strength that comes from discovering He enjoys you. He longs for you to experience the joy beaming from His face when He looks at you. He wants to fill you with the truth that He enjoys; when you know this truth, you are completely enabled to receive His joy. He wants *His joy to be your strength.*

## Joy from God's Face in the Bible

Israel knew the strength that came from the Lord's joy, so they kept asking God for the privilege to see His face. Their desire to have God look at them was expressed in their prayer, *"May God cause his face to shine upon us"* (Psalm 67:1) and *"Lift up the light of your countenance upon us"* (Psalm 4:6). God's covenant people longed for face-to-face intimacy with God, but this intimacy was desired by God first. God directed the high priest (Numbers 6:22-27) to pronounce this blessing upon the people. It was *God's idea that we see his happy face.*

Both God and we have a mutual desire for face-to-face relationship. These prayers show Israel's desire to be enjoyed by God. They loved to see an expression on the face of God that was beaming with delight when he looked at them. Man's opportunity to see God's face under the Mosaic covenant, completely expands in the New Covenant: *"But we all, with unveiled face, beholding as in a mirror the glory of the Lord, are being transformed into the same image from glory to glory, just as by the Spirit of the Lord"* (2 Corinthians 3:18).

David had a similar experience with the face of God. For David, the delight he experienced in the presence of God was so intense it became the top priority of his life. David said:

> *One thing I have desired of the LORD,*
> *That will I seek:*
> *That I may dwell in the house of the LORD*
> *All the days of my life,*
> *To behold the beauty of the LORD,*
> *And to inquire in His temple* (Psalm 27:4).

> *When You said, "Seek My face,"*
> *My heart said to You, "Your face, LORD, I will seek."*
> *Do not hide Your face from me* (Psalm 27:8-9).

David was addicted to the majestic beauty of God and the delight radiating from His face. In Psalm 34:5 we see that David was so transformed by his experience with God's face that he exhorts us, *"they looked to him and were radiant, and their faces were not ashamed."* Apparently, God's radiant joy causes our face to beam with the same radiance so there is no hanging our head in shame. Through His atoning work, Jesus exchanges our shame for His dignity.

## You Were Born to Be Enjoyed

In a healthy family, a newborn infant brings great joy to his or her parents. A nurse in the hospital, handing our newborn son to us for the first time, said, "Here is your little bundle of joy."

A baby is fully enjoyed by its parents before he or she is mature, productive or has achieved anything. The family dotes on a newborn because of the sheer joy they bring. Even though the child is a huge inconvenience, consumes without producing and is a constant drain on resources, the parents consider the child a gift.

The happy couple conceived their baby because they couldn't contain their joy for one another. With irrepressible joy, it was necessary for them to enlarge their family so more people could experience this joy. So, a baby is conceived in joy, and then they become the object of their parents' joy.

Likewise, this is why God created people. There was joy in heaven that the Godhead could not contain, so they created us so we could be invited in to heaven's party. And just like a healthy parent, God enjoys you at every stage of your maturing; you are the object of God's delight at every stage of your journey.

Unfortunately, no human family accurately or fully reflects the amazing supernatural health that exists in the Godhead. The mutual delight between Father and Son in the Godhead is so glorious it is beyond human comprehension. But Jesus prayed, prior to His death, that we be given the same glory (relational health) that has existed for eternity between Father and Son. Jesus said:

"I do not pray for these alone, but also for those who will believe in Me through their word; that they all may be one, as You, Father, *are* in Me, and I in You; that they also may be one in Us, that the world may believe that You sent Me. And *the glory which You gave Me I have given them, that they may be one just as We are one*: I in

5

them, and You in Me; that they may be made perfect in one, and that the world may know that You have sent Me, and have loved them as You have loved Me. *"Father, I desire that they also whom You gave Me may be with Me where I am, that they may behold My glory which You have given Me; for You loved Me before the foundation of the world"* (John 17:20-24, italics added).

This is great news! Even though not every human family is healthy, we have now been given full access to the enormous health of heaven. All the unity, love and mutual delight that Jesus enjoyed with His Father is now available to you and I! Jesus has a word for the unity, love and mutual delight He and His Father enjoy; that word is "glory," and Jesus prays that we get all His glory!

This glory is so powerful that it divinely restores health back to every broken heart; every heart that has experienced the inferior "glory" of human relationships.

You were designed to be enjoyed by God, and because of this, nothing else will satisfy you. But praise God, because the one who has designed you to be enjoyed has not left your longing unfulfilled.

The Lord simplified the Ten Commandments for us. He instructed us to love God and love people.

This command is easier said than practiced, since you can't give what you don't have. You can't obey even this simplified set of commands by drawing on the strength of your own will or ability. God is not expecting you to grit your teeth and try harder in your own ability to love people.

*God wants to radically and supernaturally equip you to receive His love to enable you to radically and supernaturally love people.*

God considers you infinitely valuable, and He enjoys you and takes great delight in you! As you begin to realize how God see's you, this truth about your true identity transforms your heart.

The transformation that comes from discovering your identity equips you to love people. You find yourself *giving* love more effectively because you are now *receiving* love more effectively.

You discover a lifestyle of loving people that organically flows out of who you are. This lifestyle is joyful and vastly superior to your old habit of functioning like a duty-driven worker, trying to love people in your own ability.

God's love will begin to overflow your heart and touch the lives of others when you are not even trying. You find yourself honoring, valuing and loving people because *you* are receiving the honor, value and love God has for you!

You are beginning to *act like* Jesus because you have discovered
that *you are like* Jesus. That is, you are made in His image
(Genesis 1:26 and 2 Corinthians 3:18).

# CHAPTER 2

# God Redeemed You Because He Enjoys You

G od created you in order to enjoy you, and if you were taken from Him, He is will not easily give up this source of His joy. The Gospel from man's perspective is good news. Jesus restores our relationship with God by His work on the cross. But the Gospel from God's perspective is equally magnificent. God is not willing to forever forfeit relationship with the ones who He has enjoyed from the beginning. He is simply not willing to be left forever without the ones He enjoys. If anything happens that threatens to block relationship with you, He is determined to remove the barrier no matter what it costs Him.

The entire Bible can be viewed in three parts:

- God is a Father who wanted a family (Genesis 1-2)
- God lost His kids (Genesis 3)
- God wants His kids back (Genesis 3-Revelation 22)

In Genesis 3, while Adam is hiding from God and attempting to cover his sin, God is coming toward Adam with a plan already in place to restore relationship! God want His kids back!

God is a Father who loves His kids so much that if one of us gets kidnapped, He will do everything in His power to get us back. Most parents would be willing to lose their life if that's what it took to find and rescue a kidnapped child. The parents of a kidnapped child are tormented day and night until the child is found. There is much rejoicing when a kidnapped child is found safe, rescued and returned to his parents.

The recovery of a lost child and the subsequent rejoicing when the child is found is exactly the subject of Luke chapter 15. The father in this parable can't wait to rejoice when his lost son is found.

God is not aloof, bored or detached when He considers relationship with you. He is not content to sit around in a comfortable house, indifferent to your return. Jesus left heaven's comfort zone with one passionate, determined mission: to rescue lots of "sons." He considered you and I so valuable that He choose to die rather than live without us! On the way to the cross, even though He was enduring massive mistreatment and dishonor, He focused instead on "the joy that was set before Him" (Hebrews 12:2), which is you and I! God redeemed you because He enjoys you!

He is diligently pursuing lost coins and lost sheep and passionately rejoices when they are found. He is looking out the window everyday longing for the return of His prodigal son, and then sprinting towards him to embrace him!

The story of the prodigal son in Luke 15 is the story of an enormously benevolent, forgiving father. After the prodigal son left home to pursue vain fulfilment, his father could not stop thinking about the joy and anticipation of his son's return. He would let his son follow his own longings, but would never lose his desire for restored relationship.

The father never loses the sense of his prodigal son's value, even though the son was busy displaying uniformly bad behavior. The joy the father has felt for his son since the day he was born is somehow undiminished by his son's poor choices.

As the prodigal son sheepishly returns home, full of shame, he is anticipating a less than joyful reception. He has dishonored his father, lost all his money, pursued self-indulgence and ended up in the pig pen.

The prodigal son develops a "repentance speech," hoping the father will accept him back as a servant; he believes his shameful behavior has disqualified him from the privilege of being a son.

As he nears his family's home, he is surprised at the sight of his father running toward him. The father can't contain his joy at his boy's return! He envelops him in a bear hug even though he must have still reeked with the stench of the pig pen.

The father doesn't make a single reference to the son's bad behavior and doesn't even let his boy complete his repentance speech. This happy father is focused only on restoring his son's dignity and all the privileges of being a son. The father calls for his "best robe" to be brought to cover over the pig-stained clothing – an exchange for the son's shame for the father's dignity. This is a picture of the "robe of righteousness God gives us in exchange for our filthy rags" (Isaiah 61:10, 64:6). Next, the father calls for a ring and sandals. The ring placed on the son's hand is an emblem of fully restored family authority. The sandals provide a "new" source of protection for the son's walk and a renewed sense of purpose for the son's life; this renewed life is far more noble and respectable than his previous pursuit of self-indulgence. His father can't contain his joy, so he spares no expense in planning for an extravagant party to celebrate his son's return.

If you survey the entire chapter of Luke 15, a distinct theme emerges about our Heavenly Father's heart: He likes to celebrate when lost things are recovered, and He can't contain His joy when relationship with lost children is restored. In Luke 15 the action of rejoicing is mentioned 11 times. God is an enormously benevolent, forgiving Father who diligently searches for "lost sons" so He can throw a party in heaven to celebrate restored relationship.

Jesus is the new covenant door to the Father, making possible this joyful reunion between man and God! But is it possible God has throughout history been joyfully standing at a covenant door of salvation for his people? This subject came up in a recent discussion with a friend of mine, Osil Pistole. Osil is a very joyful person, and people often take notice. Because joy is one of her core characteristics, she was inspired to study the verse in Nehemiah 8:10, *"The joy of the Lord is your strength!"* She began to ask herself, "what does Nehemiah 8:10 actually mean? How does the Lord's joy give us strength? Below is what she discovered.

First, let's look at the historical context of this Bible event recorded by Nehemiah. The newly freed Israelites were rebuilding their lives within the new walls of Jerusalem. Israel had been in slavery and exile for 70 years, so most of the returning Israelites had never even set foot in their homeland. As a matter of fact, unless they were over the age of 70, they had never heard the Law read until this very moment when they all gathered in front of the Water Gate to hear Ezra read the ancient scriptures.

It was a very dramatic moment. As the Law was being read, Israel was overwhelmed with the shame of their broken covenant with God, and they burst out weeping. The sudden conviction in their hearts of God's holiness and their sinfulness, mixed with the celebration of the end of their captivity, was too much to bear.

*The intensity of their shame threatened to overpower their celebration of freedom.*

In response, Nehemiah became acutely aware of the heart of the Lord for this situation. The people were ashamed, and God wanted to encourage them! So, God instructed the people to stop mourning and weeping, and instead to start celebrating what the Lord had done. This is where we are introduced to this most amazing phrase when (in Nehemiah 8:10) Nehemiah says,

*"Go and enjoy choice food and sweet drinks, and send some to those who have nothing prepared. This day is holy to our Lord. Do not grieve, for the joy of the Lord is your strength."*

Soon, the sounds of joy, song, and laughter arose within the walls of the city, as a healing balm covering the sounds of horror from the captivity 70 years earlier, re-establishing the dominion of the rule of the Kingdom within the land.

To understand the power of that phrase, it is important to recognize the meaning behind that particular word for joy:

The original Hebrew for "joy" in Nehemiah 8:10 is "*chedvah,*» meaning joy or gladness.

This word is only used twice in Scripture, both related to Yahweh's joy. Besides Nehemiah 8:10, it is also used in 1 Chronicles 16 when the ark is brought into David's tabernacle and the Levites sing a song of praise celebrating that the symbol of the covenant was once again in their midst.

*"Splendor and majesty are before him; strength and joy are in his dwelling place."*

(1 Chronicles 16:27)

In Nehemiah 8 and 1 Chronicles 16, the joy of the Lord is the expression of God's heart when He reaffirms His intimate relationship with Israel based on His rock-solid faithfulness to His covenant. Their tendency is to focus on the shame of their failure; God wants to refocus Israel on His joy for their relationship!

In the Hebrew language, every letter has its own meaning, so the true meaning of the word becomes evident when we put the meanings of each letter together:

*Chedvah* is a noun derived from the verb *chadah* (meaning: to rejoice). The Hebrew consonants are chet-dalet-hey.

The *chet* means a wall or fence. The *dalet* means a door. *Hey* means to look or behold. Together, the picture these three letters in *CHADAH* present is: "Behold, a door in the wall." If a wall has no door, the wall is merely an object of separation. But this Hebrew word indicates God wants us to behold (focus on) the *door* instead of the *wall*. He doesn't want His people feeling disqualified because of their failure. He doesn't want them standing on the other side of a wall from Him. He is redirecting our focus so we can see Him joyfully standing at the open covenant door He has built into the wall. He isn't blocked by the wall of our failure; He is focused on the joy of restoring relationship with us. His joy of being with us is the revelation that brings strength to our hearts.

*Dalet* is an interesting character, because in ancient Hebrew culture, to pass through a doorway was an act of coming into covenant with the leader of the home. So not only does dalet represent "a way in," but it also means a way into covenant with someone.

Now we can see what Yahweh's joy truly is! The joy of the Lord is His gladness in providing "a door in the wall" to enter into covenant with Him. He finds pure joy in providing the way for us to come into His presence and fellowship with Him! This was his desire from the beginning: to live in a covenant relationship with mankind! Ever since Eden, God desired family! He established Eden as a place where we could live together with Him and enjoy each other's company! After Eden, we see that God, again and again, creates "doors in the wall" through different covenants. God has always been in pursuit of man, and He continues to pursue every single human being ever created.

Under the Mosaic Covenant, the door was the Law. Now we have a new door! Jesus is the door! In John 10:7, Jesus said, *"Truly, truly, I say to you, 'I am the door of the sheep.'"* Again, a couple of verses after, He repeats, *"I am the door. If anyone enters by me, he will be saved and will go in and out and find pasture"* (John 10:9).

So, what makes the Lord happy? The Lord rejoices that there is a door for us to come into fellowship with Him. The joy of Lord is that He is able to enjoy being with us! The joy of the Lord is us!

The author of Hebrews clarifies this even more for us: *"For the joy set before him he endured the cross, scorning its shame, and sat down at the right hand of the throne of God"* (Hebrews 12:2). As a matter of fact, tradition tells us that as part of Passover in ancient Israel, Jesus would likely have been singing Psalm 118 on His way to the Garden where He would shortly be arrested, then prosecuted, and crucified, establishing the New Covenant.

*"This is the day the Lord has made; we will rejoice and be glad in it."*

(Psalm 118:24)

Those were the words on our Savior's lips as He went forth to become our forever door to fellowship with God. Jesus has opened a door that never shuts; a door that is open to everyone who enters through. Jesus has removed the barrier between man and God, and He is standing at the door smiling!

## A Double Miracle

In winter some years ago, during an inspection of a fast-food restaurant in Idaho, the manager and the assistant manager were on site. As I was conducting the inspection, I felt the Lord pointing out the assistant manager to me. He wanted me to encourage her. I could feel the Lord's love for her, and He showed me her sincere, unselfish heart.

It was mid-morning, and the restaurant was not busy, and so I told the managers I would like to speak a word of encouragement to the assistant. They agreed. I told her the Lord was proud of her, and that He saw her sincere, unselfish heart. I asked her if I could put my hand on her shoulder as I prayed for her. She was deeply moved by the comforting presence of the Lord, and she began to cry. As I was praying, I glanced over to the manager, and she was also crying. They were both experiencing the tangible presence of God and His comfort and encouragement. Then, the manager reached out to the assistant manager and the two hugged as they cried.

After a few minutes of this, the assistant manager told me her story. This had been one of the worst mornings of her life. She had been experiencing significant difficulties in her marriage, and that morning her husband had been angry and verbally abusive toward her. She was distraught and overwhelmed and decided she would call in sick to work. But just before she made that phone call, she somehow felt she needed to go to work, and so she changed her mind. On her drive to work, she was feeling deeply sad, ashamed and hopeless. She was hoping to have enough emotional strength to get through the day.

When she got to work, she was trying to set her emotions aside so she could concentrate on her duties. About a half an hour later, I entered the restaurant. As she was listening to my word of encouragement for her, she was moved to tears because the Lord's hope and comfort were displacing her grief and pain. She told me, "Today began as one of the worst days of my life, and I am so surprised to be so miraculously comforted and encouraged!"

It turns out that the manager and assistant were not just co-workers but they were good friends. The manager was a good listener and a source of emotional support to her assistant manager. The assistant manager was a Christian, and she had been praying for her manager to be able to experience the love of Jesus in a way that inspired her to receive Jesus.

The manager was visibly moved by the love and presence of the Lord as I prayed and prophesied over her assistant manager. She had never seen such a dramatic example of God's love in action. She was marveling at what just happened. She was still wiping away tears. Because I could see her heart was wide open to the Lord, I invited her to talk with me privately in her office. She knew the prophetic word was accurate for her friend, and she wanted to ask me some questions. As we talked, I felt prompted to explain the Gospel to her. I told her the Lord's love for her friend was also available for her. I told her God is a warm-hearted Father who loves her. I told her, "God has done everything in His power to make relationship with you possible, and He is just waiting for you to say yes." Then I asked, "Do you want to say yes to relationship with God?" Without hesitation, she answered yes. So, I led her in a prayer to receive the Lord, and we walked out of her office.

When the assistant manager found out her manager friend had just received the Lord, she was overjoyed. She had been praying this would happen for several years. That day, the Lord did a double miracle: He supernaturally comforted and encouraged a woman in her day of despair, and then He answered her prayer for the salvation of her good friend. When I left that restaurant, all three of us were rejoicing in God's goodness!

This is another true-life story that confirms God views people in their unredeemed state as an infinitely valuable lost child. He is determined to pursue us, redeem us and invite us into the celebration as empowered sons and daughters!

# CHAPTER 3

# Empowered Sons

God is an extravagantly loving Father who adopts us into His family; this adoption redefines our identity as we discover His joy for us. God is also a King. He sovereignly rules the earth and imparts favor and authority to those who are surrendered to Him. Receiving love from God as Father empowers us to surrender to God as King.

The unconditional love of God as Father wins our heart and inspires our surrender. As we posture ourself in full surrender, we position ourself to receive His favor and authority to change the world. Jesus points us toward the Father to be empowered by His love, and then He points us outward to join Him in His epic quest to bring His Kingdom on earth.

## Something Is Different

For several years, I had been inspecting a certain fast-food restaurant and had developed a good working relationship with the managers. I had interacted with them as a health inspector, but I had never felt prompted to use my prophetic gift until this day. The assistant manager was walking with me during this inspection. She was a

Hispanic woman in her mid-thirties. As I looked at her, something was different about her, something new I hadn't noticed before.

This visit quickly changed from a routine health inspection to a prophetic encounter. Suddenly, I was aware someone had been powerfully praying for this assistant manager. In the previous six times I had visited this restaurant, she did not seem receptive to the love of Jesus, but I had a strong sense that she was very receptive now.

I asked her a question: "What's different about you?" She said, "What do you mean?" So, I asked, "Who has been praying for you?" She immediately replied, "It is my mother; she has been praying for me consistently for many years." I told her, "Wow, I can feel the power of her prayers! You need to thank her for praying for you, because your heart has recently become very receptive to the love of the Lord." Then, I asked her, "Does that sound true to you?" She agreed, "Yes."

I asked the manager if I could spend a few minutes talking with her assistant in the dining room. She gave me permission, and so I asked the assistant manager if she wanted to hear more about Jesus' love for her. We sat down in the dining room and talked for about 15 minutes. I explained the Gospel, with an emphasis on the Father's desire for relationship with her. She was receptive.

As I was explaining to her how simple it was to receive the Lord, I felt the Lord redirect me. He told me to write down my prophetic word for her and write out a specific prayer for her that would serve as a guide for her to receive the Lord. I think the Lord knew she might feel obligated to pray the pray with me in the dining room because I was the health inspector. The Lord wanted her decision to receive Him to be her free-will choice. So, God was removing all pressure she might feel to please *me*.

For the next 15 minutes, I sat at the dining room table and wrote out what the Lord had instructed me to do. I completed the inspection, thanked her for her time, and left the restaurant.

About six months later, I walked through the side door of this restaurant to perform another inspection. As soon as the assistant manager saw me, she began to run toward me with childlike enthusiasm. She ran up, gave me a hug and told me her whole life had changed. She said she had taken my note home and had prayed the prayer to receive Jesus. After praying this prayer, she felt joy. After praying, she explained what she had done to her husband, and he wanted to receive the Lord also. She told me her conversion had inspired her family and extended family and many of them were coming to Christ.

She told me her family was deeply grateful to me, and they had all found a home church and were happy there. She said she had been waiting for a few months for me to visit her restaurant so she could tell me the good news. She said her family refer to me as "the man of God who visits restaurants." I was overjoyed at how the Lord had dramatically intervened in the life of this family!

This story demonstrates once again how my experiencing the love of God then naturally flowed outward to touch and transform multiple generations!

**Inward and Outward**

In John 7:37-38, Jesus is instructing us to face inward, and then outward:

*"On the last day, that great day of the feast, Jesus stood and cried out, saying, "If anyone thirsts, let him come to Me and drink. He who*

*believes in Me, as the Scripture has said, out of his heart will flow rivers of living water."*

If we move toward Jesus and drink from His love, His love will expand inside us and begin to flow outward; it will become a well of life for others around us. This is exactly what happened to the Samaritan woman in John 4:1-26. Jesus, the well of love for humanity, is sitting on a well. When Jesus encounters the woman at the well, He invites her to experience His love, and as she drinks, she becomes a well of life for her whole community (John 4:39-42).

Our ability to be spiritually fruitful is empowered by Christ's love. He invites us to drink from His love and become a well of life for others. Our ability to fully surrender to God as King is also empowered by God's love. The Father invites us to experience His affection for us in a way that empowers us to surrender.

**Come Unto Me**

The Lord has designed you to need Him. Jesus points you to Himself as the one who fulfills many of your God-given desires:

**For thirst**: *"If anyone thirsts, let him come to Me and drink"* (John 7:37).

**For rest**: *"Come to Me, all you who labor and are heavy laden, and I will give you rest"* (Matthew 11:28).

**For hunger and thirst**: *"I am the bread of life. He who comes to Me shall never hunger, and he who believes in Me shall never thirst"* (John 6:35).

**For truth and life**: *"Jesus said to him, "I am the way, the truth, and the life. No one comes to the Father except through Me"* (John 14:6).

**For eternal life**: *"Jesus said to her, "I am the resurrection and the life. He who believes in Me, though he may die, he shall live"* (John 11:25).

**For spiritual fruit**: *"I am the vine, you are the branches. He who abides in Me, and I in him, bears much fruit; for without Me you can do nothing"* (John 15:5).

We go to the Lord to find love, truth, freedom, strength, and wholeness. His plan is to impart Himself *to* us so He can impart Himself *through* us. We go *to* the Lord for wholeness, and then as we mature, we go *with* the Lord in ministry. Like a divine romance, our Bridegroom fully includes us in the two-dimensional journey of knowing Him. He invites us first to intimacy, and then to partnership. Empowered by His love, we join Him in His epic quest to change the world.

## Jesus Moved In Authority Because He Was Submitted to Authority

The Lord calls us inward for personal wholeness, and then calls us outward to extend His Kingdom. Our Father wants healthy sons who share his purpose. He loves us unconditionally and redefines our identity through the lens of His affection for us. Once we have become healthy sons, He is motivated to transfer His favor and authority to us, which empowers us to change the world.

Jesus is the beloved Son who is motivated by love to surrender His Father's will. Jesus does nothing on His own initiative; He lets His Father take the lead. In doing so, Jesus sets an example for us.

Having received the extravagant love of His Father, Jesus is inspired to surrender to the Father's will. Because Jesus submits His will to the will of the Father, He is aligning Himself with authority so he can operate with authority.

This shows an important truth: you can only have authority if you can submit to authority. The biblical principle of having authority comes from submitting to authority is illustrated in Matthew 8:5-10:

*"When Jesus entered the village of Capernaum, a captain in the Roman army approached him, asking for a miracle. 'Lord,' he said, 'I have a son who is lying in my home, paralyzed and suffering terribly.'"* (TPT)

*Jesus responded, 'I will go with you and heal him.'*

*But the Roman officer interjected, 'Lord, who am I to have you come into my house? <u>I understand your authority</u>, for I too am a man who walks under authority and have authority over soldiers who serve under me. I can tell one to go and he'll go, and another to come and he'll come. I command my servants and they'll do whatever I ask. So, I know that all you need to do is to stand here and command healing over my son and he will be instantly healed.'*

*Jesus was astonished when he heard this and said to those who were following him, 'He has greater faith than anyone I've encountered in Israel!'"*

The Roman captain recognizes Jesus has authority because He walks under authority. Notice how he says to Jesus, *"I understand your authority*, for I too am a man who walks under authority and have authority"* (Matthew 8:8). Jesus was astonished at the Roman captain's faith. This centurion's faith was greater than any in Israel because he understood how authority flows in God's Kingdom.

## Jesus Wants to Give You Authority

Jesus was fully submitted to the Father's will in going to the cross. Because He displayed ultimate submission at the cross, He now moves in ultimate authority after His resurrection.

What does Jesus do with all authority? Immediately after His resurrection, Jesus is imparting authority to His disciples, empowering them to accomplish His purpose:

Matthew 28:18-19, *"And Jesus came and spoke to them, saying, 'All authority has been given to Me in heaven and on earth. Go therefore and make disciples of all the nations, baptizing them in the name of the Father and of the Son and of the Holy Spirit.'"*

When we are young, He pulls us towards Him to embrace us with His unconditional and extravagant love. His affection and acceptance become the foundation of our identity. As we mature in His love, His love inspires and empowers our surrender. You could picture God much like medieval kings would have been, although He is also a loving Father.

A Son has been inspired by His Father's love to surrender to his Father (who is also a King). A healthy Son has matured into a "knight." The Father's love has given him identity, purpose and courage. Now the Son (as a Knight) has the strength to bow before God (as King). The King transfers His authority to His son to extend His Kingdom in the earth.

My prayer for you is that God's love for you as Father will inspire your surrender to God as King! God intends you to be His beloved son and his powerful knight!

# CHAPTER 4

# Empowered by God's Presence

The joy of the Lord is our strength. Put another way, we are infused with divine strength as we are enjoyed by God. If we lose our strength, we will give up, or we may try to carry out God's will in our own strength.

## The Source of Our Strength

If we lose intimacy with God, we will try to build His Kingdom according to our own design instead of His. God has designed us to need Him, because He wants sons who are creative partners, not just servants who are only duty-driven workers. It is impossible to maintain the strength to obey God without the joy of being *with* God.

If we could be entirely successful without being close to God, then we would not need Him at all for success. So, He has designed us so that *we can't succeed without being close to Him, because He originally created us as the objects of His joy.* What good is it to create companions if they have no need for companionship? He will not deny Himself the pleasure of being close to us, but He has given us free will; we must *choose* to be close to Him. When we choose to be close to Him, His joy becomes our strength. Being filled with His joy gives us the strength we need to be His creative partner. Living then becomes an exciting daily adventure as the Holy Spirit leads us.

## Choosing to Give Thanks

Some years ago, my wife and I were enjoying a Christmas meal with our extended family. I was expecting some pleasant, informal family time and not to operate in any spiritual gifts or to do any ministry. As I was eating my turkey and stuffing, I glanced over and saw a distant relative of mine named Mike. Mike was much thinner than I had remembered. He was struggling to chew and swallow his food.

I felt a tangible wave of compassion wash over me. I could feel God's profound love for this man. Not knowing much of anything about his present circumstances or his past history, all I knew was God was empowering me to encourage him. Since there were several dozen people eating in a relatively small living room, I decided to ask Mike if I could pray for him in the guest bedroom area.

Mike and his sister Michelle followed me into the guest bedroom. I sat on the side of the small bed and they sat on the carpet facing me. As I began to pray and bless Mike, I could feel the increased flow of God's compassion for him. As I continued to pray, the Lord showed me a detailed visual image of Mike. I saw Mike in a car, covered with several blankets. It was about sunrise, and he was just waking up. I could tell he was physically uncomfortable. He appeared weak, cold, hungry and in pain. Right after he awoke, he sat up and began to pray. I could see the pain on his face as he began to pray. Then, I became aware of the content of his prayer: he was giving thanks! He was starting his day in pain, but he was expressing a heart overflowing with thanksgiving!

I described to Mike what God was showing me. As I was talking, Mike let out a loud scream! He said, "No, no, no!" Then he turned to his sister, Michelle, and said, "Did you tell him that?" Mike didn't believe what he was hearing, because I was perfectly describing what he had been doing every morning.

What I didn't know is that Mike was homeless. He had been living out of his car in the winter. Because of addictions, he had been estranged from his wife and family. He didn't have enough food to eat. He was suffering from cancer of his jaw or throat. He was sad, cold, sick, lonely, and in pain. He had nothing tangible to give God thanks for.

But he was rising every morning to give thanks to God! This was a heroic expression of sacrificial thanksgiving. God was so moved by Mike's thankfulness that He couldn't wait to tell him! God was proud of Mike for choosing to give thanks when there was seemingly nothing to be thankful for. God was deeply moved with compassion and love for Mike, and He wanted mike to experience how he felt about him. God was not defining Mike by his past mistakes or disqualifying him for his weakness or immaturity.

This is the first time Mike had experienced the gift of prophecy. Mike couldn't believe God actually saw him in his loneliness and affliction. That's why he screamed out the word, "No!" His first thought was he was being tricked because his sister had given me his private information. The level of detail in that word of knowledge for Mike would have been embarrassing, if it wasn't motivated by compassion. Mike's first thought was I might be using privileged information to trick him, but Mike was having a profound encounter with the outrageous goodness of God.

This encounter for Mike was the beginning of a comprehensive transformation in Mike's life. He reconciled with his family, recovered from his addiction, his cancer went into remission and he was able to get meaningful employment.

Mike desperately needed to encounter the love of God, and God showed up for him! He needed to know God saw him and cared about him. He needed to know God saw goodness in him. He needed to know he wasn't disqualified by the mistakes of his past. He needed God to prepare the path ahead of him and bless his future. And God met him at his point of need in every area.

As I was empowered by God's presence that day a door opened in Mike's heart and he encountered Christ his Redeemer. This man walked away eternally changed and with a joy and peace he never knew was possible.

## Jesus Wants You to Experience His Joy

Jesus wants you to experience His joy, but how? By granting you access to the glory of the Godhead. Giving us full access to His joy is the central theme of His request as He prayed to the Father in John chapter 17. *"But now I come to You, and these things I speak in the world, that they may have My joy fulfilled in themselves"* (John 17:13).

As Jesus continues to pray, He expresses His heart cry for the church at a critical time – at the end of His ministry on earth. His prayer to the Father shows us His highest priority as He is about to leave earth: to *grant us full access to all the glory, love and unity that the Godhead has been enjoying for eternity.* What an awesome privilege for mankind! Jesus doesn't want us to be left out of anything that He has been enjoying in His relationship with the Father.

At the time of His prayer, Jesus is looking forward to returning to heaven where He can again experience the original glory of an un-distracted relationship with his Father. In His earthly ministry, Jesus perfectly represented His Father, but the nature of their relationship was different. Jesus was focused on completing His mission on earth. In this prayer, we see Jesus expressing His desire to resume the former glory that He had with His Father before the world was created.

The glory Jesus is referring to in John 17:5 is not merely His individual glory, as King Jesus returning to His throne. *"And now, O Father, glorify Me together with Yourself, with the glory which I had with You before the world was."*

The glory Jesus is talking about is the glory of *relationship between Father and Son*. Something was especially glorious about their relationship, and it took both of them to fully display it. So, Jesus says, "Glorify me *together with yourself*, with the glory I had *with you* before the world was" (italics added).

This relational glory with the Father brings Jesus such joy; He desires the same level of joy for us. Jesus loves us so much that He refuses to exclude us from the supreme level of divine joy previously available only to the Godhead. So, Jesus prays for us, *"that they may have My joy fulfilled in themselves"* (John 17:13).

Jesus further asks the Father to give us the full, undiminished dose of glory and love that He has been receiving from the Father (John 17:22-23). Every shred of the love and honor that the Father eternally radiates toward Jesus now gets focused in our direction – because of Jesus' prayer!

Jesus wants to position us toward Him so we can absorb all the majestic splendor that radiates from Him (John 17:24-26). This glory shines so brightly from Jesus that it illuminates anything in its path, imparting an equal and undiminished glory to us. We get to experience His full brightness, not a toned-down version.

The Godhead is like a solar system that attracts us into its gravitational field. Jesus grants us full access to a superior orbit. The Father, like the sun, is the origin of glory. The Father is forever beaming forth the full brightness and energy of His love and delight for Jesus.

Jesus is like a planet that rotates around His father and absorbs the full glory of His Father's light beam. Somehow, no energy is lost.

By absorbing the full glory continuously, the Son is equally as brilliant, majestic and glorious as His Father. And finally, Jesus magnetically attracts us by His love, and then focuses the full force of that love on us. Jesus effectively absorbs the entirety of His Father's love, and then directs an undiminished version of that that love to us. Jesus says, *"I have loved them (us) as You (Father) have loved Me"* (John 17:13). How could Jesus have given us a more awesome privilege than to absorb the full glory of love that has forever existed in the Godhead?

Jesus' foremost desire at the end of His ministry is to bring us into the relational bliss of the Godhead. He wants to provide us unrestricted access to the healthiest, most mutually delightful relationship that has ever existed.

Twice in his prayer, Jesus requests something that has existed from the age before time. He is referring to the eternal and original relationship between Father and Son. First, Jesus asks His Father to return the glory Jesus had "before the world began" (John 17:4). Jesus had obeyed His Father's will on earth, but now He longs to return to the unhindered state of relational bliss He has enjoyed with His Father for eternity.

Second, Jesus wants us to receive the glory He radiates to us and realize this glory had its origin in His Father's love for Him. Jesus said, *"that they may behold My glory which You have given Me; for You loved Me before the foundation of the world"* (John 17:24). Jesus wants us to look at Him so we can receive the undiminished version of divine love that He has been continually absorbing from His father.

## CHAPTER 5

# The Healthiest Relationship

In order to discover what Jesus is giving us when He prayed for us to receive His glory, we must discover the nature of the glorious relationship enjoyed by the Heavenly Father and the Son that existed *before the foundation of the world.* Twice in His prayer, Jesus refers to the glory and bliss He enjoyed with the Father before the world began (John 17:5 and John 17:24). The same glorious relational bliss in the Godhead is now available to us because of Jesus' prayer.

How do we discover the nature of the glorious relationship enjoyed by the Heavenly Father and the Son that existed from before the world began? Scripture gives us a glimpse. Although it may seem like an obscure passage, Proverbs 8:22-31 pulls aside the veil on eternity and shows us the exact nature of the ancient glory that has forever existed between the Father and Son.

Proverbs 8 reveals the *prototype* Father and Son relationship. It is the healthiest, most mutually delightful relationship that has ever existed. This relationship provides the perfect pattern for how we are intended to interact with God as His children.

The passage begins with verses that show the Son of God is eternal and has been with his Father forever (vs. 22-29). These verses reveal that there was a close creative collaboration between the Father and His Son during the act of creation. They were creative partners. But it is the next two verses which speak volumes about the nature of their relationship.

Jesus makes this statement: *"Then I was beside Him as a master craftsman; and, I was daily His delight, rejoicing always before Him, Rejoicing in His inhabited world, and my delight was with the sons of men"* (Proverbs 8:30-31).

If you look closely, you see that the Godhead had different functions during the process of creation. The Father functioned like an architect, planning creation, and the Son functioned as a builder, declaring and carrying out His Father's wishes. Jesus refers to himself as a *"master craftsman"* (vs. 30). Jesus, as His Father's creative partner, was a highly skilled master artisan who turned all His Father's creative ideas into functional works of art. A craftsman is both highly skilled and also takes the time necessary to create something of great beauty. The work of creation was not rushed or performed under pressure to meet deadlines. The world was intended to be a place for humans to inhabit, but it also displayed the vast genius of the divine Master Designer and Artist.

The design studio of heaven resembled a party between Father and Son more than a workplace in which workers focus on completing tasks. As Jesus was by His Father's side, crafting the world, He said, *"daily I was my father's delight, and I was rejoicing always before him"* (vs. 30). This creative partnership between Father and Son had more focus on *mutual delight* than on accomplishing a goal. The Father and Son were not in a hurry, and they placed a high value on enjoying each other in process.

And yet, the achievement of creation is magnificent and is by no means shoddy work. With no pressure to perform, and in a context of constant mutual delight and rejoicing, the Father and the Son created a masterpiece! In two verses describing the process of creation, the words "delight" and "rejoicing" are used twice. Jesus was so overjoyed at both the creative process and His finished product, He couldn't stop rejoicing.

This relationship between the Heavenly Father and Son describes the exact nature of the relationship that God wants for us. We are not just heaven's servants, born into God's family to perform tasks. We are sons of God, birthed into God's family as creative partners. We get to be co-creators with God and enjoy the experience of undiminished mutual delight that has existed between the Father and Son for eternity! Jesus wants us to experience the same glory and love that He has always enjoyed with His father, and so that is what He prayed in John 17:22-24.

## Jesus Was the Focus of His Father's Delight

I want to share a description for how the glorious relationship between Father and Son looked. As the Father and the Son partnered together in the act of creation, the Father couldn't contain His joy for His Son. Every time He looked at Jesus, His face literally radiated with bright, majestic light. This light carried a beam of joy that kept bathing Jesus in His Father's glory; a beam of joy forever focused on Jesus. This joy beam filled Jesus with so much joy He couldn't contain it. Jesus responded by rejoicing, which is what a person does when they have too much joy to contain!

For however long it took to complete creation, this festival of joy and rejoicing continued. Jesus was simultaneously motivated by His Father's delight and inspired by His Father's creative idea. So, when Jesus called creation into existence, He overflowed with divine delight as He carried out His Father's will.

In fact, when it comes to joy, even though Jesus faced intense difficulties during His time on earth, He lived a lifestyle of joy.

## Jesus Lived a Lifestyle of Joy

- He continually walked in His Father's delight (Matthew 3:17).

- His heart was synchronized with His Father, so He was given the oil of joy above all people (Hebrews 1:9).

- He was motivated by His Father's joy to do His will. He said, "I delight to do your will" (Psalm 40:8). He was motivated by His Father's love to obey Him (John 15). He instructs us to abide in the Father's love so we can be motivated by God's love too.

- He was motivated by joy to redeem us (Hebrews 12:2). He was misunderstood, unjustly treated and crucified by the ones He enjoyed. In spite of all that, He didn't stop enjoying people, even though they gave Him no reason to enjoy them.

- He continued to enjoy His disciples, even though He foreknew they would all abandon or betray Him (Luke 22:14).

# CHAPTER 6

# The Focus of Jesus' Delight

What did the Father do with the fullness of joy He couldn't contain? *He focused His joy on Jesus.* Jesus received His Father's joy, and He was filled with so much joy He couldn't contain it either. As we discussed, Jesus, having more joy than He could contain, expressed His joy by rejoicing. As Jesus was rejoicing, He desired for more people to rejoice with.

> *"Then I was beside Him as a master craftsman; And I was daily His delight, rejoicing always before Him, Rejoicing in His inhabited world, and my delight was with the sons of men"* (Proverbs 8:30-31).

Not content to restrict heaven's party to just a few participants, Jesus decided to enlarge the guest list so he could rejoice with more people. But in order to do this, He needed to create something more than a magnificent planet inhabited by plants and animals. He needed to create people; people in His own image could fully appreciate the joy of the Godhead. He had to craft a special class of beings that were fully equipped first to receive, and then to express, His joy. This is great news for the human race! We exist because the

Godhead *had so much joy they couldn't contain it*, and *so we were designed as the object of God's joy*. You and I were designed to be enjoyed by God.

Marriage is an earthly example of this heavenly reality. When husband and wife express joy for one another that they cannot contain, the natural result is a child is conceived. The only way husband and wife can share their joy is to *enlarge their family*. So, a child is conceived in their image to extend this irrepressible joy beyond marriage to family.

Overflowing love needs something to love, and overflowing joy needs a person to enjoy. So, Jesus looks at us and says, *"but my delight is with the sons of men"* (Proverbs 8:31). Jesus focuses all His joy on us! The *human race is the object of the Lord's delight*. This truth is so amazing that it seems too good to be true, right? But it gets even better. Since delight is the Lord's original sentiment towards us, we don't have to earn it or work for it. It was the Lord's idea to create us for His own delight.

Joy was the Lord's motive in creating you, and joy was the Lord's motive in redeeming you: *"Looking unto Jesus, the author and finisher of our faith, who for the joy that was set before Him endured the cross, despising the shame, and has sat down at the right hand of the throne of God"* (Hebrews 12:2).

When Jesus was enduring the pain of the cross, He was not just focused on His pain; He was focused on what He would gain. Christ's death removed every obstacle that blocked relationship between Him and the ones He has delighted in since creation! So, you were created as His delight, and He overcame the pain of the cross as He focused on you as the source of His delight. *You* were the joy that was set before Jesus! His motivating force at the cross was the joy of relationship with you!

Jesus *focused on you* as His source of joy. Now, you are free *to focus on Him* as your source of joy! That is why Hebrews 12:2 starts out, *"looking unto Jesus."* As we discover *we are* His joy, then looking at Him brings *us* joy. God's motive in His epic plan of redemption was to restore our relationship to His original intent. And the original intent was mutual joy between you and Jesus.

**Transformed by His Face**

In creation, the beam of enjoyment radiating from the Father's face was focused on Jesus, and Jesus focuses His beam of enjoyment on us. This was God's original intention for man.

Adam and Eve experienced God's joy in an unhindered way until they sinned. Their sin hindered their relationship with God. Eventually, the Old Testament law was instituted, but it was not an adequate or permanent solution for restoring relationship between God and man.

God was determined to restore face-to-face relationship with man. Since the Lord created us for His own enjoyment, God would not permanently deny Himself the pleasure of intimate relationship with us. So, He sent His Son to redeem us. Jesus restored face-to-face relationship with God.

Moses' relationship with God was a prophetic foreshadowing of what God was going to make possible for *all of us* under the New Covenant:

*"But if the ministry of death, written and engraved on stones, was glorious, so that the children of Israel could not look steadily at the face of Moses because of the glory of his countenance, which glory was passing away, how will the ministry of the Spirit not be more glorious?"* (2 Corinthians 3:7-8)

Moses experienced the same beam of joy radiating from God's face that Jesus experiences and describes in Proverbs 8:30. The glory coming from God's face transformed Moses' face so much so, it glowed. Under the New Covenant, Jesus has purchased access to God's face for *all of us!*

*"But we all, with unveiled face, beholding as in a mirror the glory of the Lord, are being transformed into the same image from glory to glory, just as by the Spirit of the Lord"* (2 Corinthians 3:18).

Now, *all* humans have access by the blood of Christ to the same transforming glory coming from God's face that Jesus has enjoyed for eternity. From man's perspective, access to God's face is an awesome privilege. But from God's perspective, it is what Jesus has longed for since He created us as the object of His delight.

This is why Jesus prays this in John 17:24: "Father, I desire that they also whom You gave Me *may be with Me* where I am, *that they may behold My glory which You have given Me*; for *You loved Me before the foundation of the world"* (italics added).

Jesus has always wanted us to look at Him so we can be transformed by the glory of His delight for us. So, you have been God's joy, the focal point of heaven's delight, since creation. Now, because of Christ's redemption, you are free to enjoy it. Not only that, you and I are free to reveal God's delight to others.

**No Longer Ashamed**

I recall one particular day when I was in the kitchen area of a fast-food restaurant. I noticed a woman at the deep fat fryer cooking French fries. This woman stood out to me because of her age. She appeared to be in her mid-sixties, which is older than most entry-level fast-food employees. Every time I walked behind her in the kitchen, I felt a strong surge of the Lord in my heart. It was a feeling of enthusiasm. The Lord was highlighting her to me so I would pay attention. So, I asked the Lord what was happening, and He prompted me to pray for her. I asked the store manager for permission to talk to the employee for a few minutes. The manager said yes, and she called the woman from the fryer to an area just outside of her office.

As I began to speak to the French fry lady, I felt a surge of courage and authority arise in my heart. I could feel how valuable she was to the Lord. Her life had great significance, and her decades-long, diligent habit of praying for friends and family availed much. The Lord showed me how many people's lives had been changed and blessed because of her prayers. I saw the great value, significance and success of her life from His perspective.

As I began to speak this prophetic word to her, the Lord's tangible presence filled the space around us. She began to cry tears of joy and relief, and I saw her expression change. Her facial expression changed from anxious to relieved and joyful. Then, she spoke to me in Spanish and the manager translated for me.

She had been working at this restaurant for years, and then had decided to retire in her early-sixties. For several years, she had been trying to live with a very limited retirement income, and had recently concluded it was not enough for her. So, she decided her only option was to return to work, and this was only her first week back working at the fast-food restaurant. She had plenty of experience, but the manager assigned her to work at the French fry station – a task for an entry level employee. As she was working, she felt an overwhelming sense of shame.

She felt sad and ashamed of not having enough money. She felt sad and ashamed of having to return to work. She felt ashamed of working at the French fry station as a woman in her mid-sixties. As she was experiencing this grief and shame, she began to conclude she had little value, and the fruit of her whole life was insignificant. She kept quietly working as she endured the torment of her shame.

This is the point I entered the restaurant! She told me when I first walked behind her as she stood at the fryer, she felt a surge of the Holy Spirit, and she didn't know why. I felt the same thing. The Lord was highlighting us to each other to prompt us to interact. The Holy Spirit was leaping inside both of us to prepare us for a divine encounter.

This was all happening because the Lord was deeply moved by a woman who was being tormented and paralyzed by shame, and He wanted break the shame off her. This is why I felt both compassion for the woman and a surge of courage from the Lord. This is why the Lord showed me how valuable she was and the success of her life of prayer. I had the priceless privilege to function in the moment as an ambassador of heaven; my assignment was to encourage this woman and remove her shame.

This encounter reminds me of a portion of the passage in Isaiah 61:1-3:

*"He has sent Me to heal the brokenhearted, To proclaim liberty to the captives, and the opening of the prison to those who are bound...And the opening of the prison to those who are bound...To comfort all who mourn, To console those who mourn in Zion, To give them beauty for ashes, The oil of joy for mourning, The garment of praise for the spirit of heaviness."*

After this encounter, myself, the woman and the manager were all crying. The Holy Spirit's presence was still strongly tangible. We all were experiencing the joy of encountering the Lord. In fact, the joy of God's presence left us partially immobilized, and so we were glad the employees in the front if the kitchen were still able to work. The Lord deployed me to displace her grief with His joy. Seeing the Lord work as an epic comforter, deliverer, encourager and shame-breaker is one of my greatest privileges. I left the restaurant full of joy!

God used me not only to focus His delight on those around me, but to let them know Jesus pursues them with His love.

# CHAPTER 7

# Jesus Pursues You

In learning that we are the focus of Jesus' delight, we want to look at various historical accounts of Jesus pursuing man. He pursued Adam when he sinned. He pursued the Shulamite because He enjoys her. He enjoys the Shulamite (drawn away), and then He runs with her to subdue the enemy and rescue the bride. He awakened the Shulamite; we are like His sleeping beauty. He pursued the prodigal son. He pursues lost people because He enjoys them: Luke 15. He pursued the woman at the well. He pursued the ten virgins to awaken a sleeping bride. He is the lion that pursues. He is a bridegroom who rejoices to run the race. For the Joy that was set before Him He redeemed us. For the Son of Man has come to *seek* and save that which is lost: Luke 19:10. Jesus masters the lifestyle of joy in a joyless world.

**The Gospel is Really Good News!**

We need to understand why God *created* us before we can understand why he *redeemed* us:

- The Godhead experiences mutual delight and joy they cannot contain.

Proverbs 8:30, "Then I was the craftsman at his side.

*I was filled with delight day after day, rejoicing always in his presence."*

- Jesus is so full of joy as a response to His Father enjoying Him that He focuses His joy on the human race. People were created because the Godhead had too much joy to keep it to themselves. People were created as intimate companions and creative partners with God. People were created to uniquely participate in a heaven's culture of intense mutual joy and creativity. In short, heaven's party was so good, God created a class of beings that could enjoy it with him. People were created as the object of God's joy.

Proverbs 8:31, "...*rejoicing in his whole world and delighting in mankind."*

- Man is created and placed in an ideal environment that is the perfect backdrop for fulfilment of every desire God had designed into him. Eden's conditions were ideal for Adam's enjoyment. Most importantly, it was the place *God and man could enjoy one another*. God designed the garden with conditions that would *inspire* Adam's relationship with God rather than *distract* him from God. God Himself communed with Adam in the cool of the morning. This relationship between God and Adam was the priority of every day, and was the ultimately the very reason both the Adam and garden was created.

- God values free will more than the absence of evil, because He wants man to make the *free-will choice* to love Him. So, God places the tree of the knowledge of good and evil in the garden, giving Adam the choice to disobey.

- The tree of life is in the center of the garden. As long as Adam maintained a lifestyle that kept the Tree of Life (Jesus) central, he was successful. When he allowed the other tree to distract him from the centrality of Christ in his life, he became vulnerable to temptation.

- Satan tempts Adam and Eve to sin. Feeling shame for the first time, they devised a method to cover themselves and exercise human effort to earn God's acceptance. God rejected their *self-covering*, and he killed an animal to provide a covering for them. This is the first example in scripture that foreshadows the death of Christ on the cross to cleanse us of sin. An innocent animal has to die to pay the price for Adam's sin in order to remove his shame. Only God can cleanse us and remove our shame. We can't do it for ourselves! We need a Savior, and we can't save ourselves! When Jesus died, the veil that separated God from man was torn from the top down!

- God takes the initiative to cleanse and redeem us because He *wouldn't **deny himself** the pleasure of being with us!*

We are that valuable to Him! He could not bear the thought of being forever isolated from us. He created us as the object of His joy! Since we are His joy, He was willing to *go to any length to rescue us.* It is like having children who are lost. The father and mother will do anything to find them and get them back in the family. Unredeemed humans are *lost* but infinitely valuable to God!

Let us look at the enormity of God's sacrifice for us in order to get us back. He will do anything to restore us back to relationship with Him!

- Genesis 3:21, *"Also for Adam and his wife the LORD God made tunics of skin, and clothed them."*

- Genesis 15:17: God enters into blood covenant with Abram, as a burning lamp passes between the halves of the animal sacrifices. A covenant ratified in blood obligates both parties to die rather than break covenant. Abram is asleep, and Godhead ratifies the covenant by Himself, obligating Himself to die rather than break covenant. He did all this because He would rather die than live without us!

- The Passover lamb and the blood on the doorposts. *"When I see the blood, I will pass over you"* (Exodus 12).

- John 1:29, "The next day John saw Jesus coming toward him, and said, '*Behold! The Lamb of God who takes away the sin of the world!'*"

- 1 Peter 1:18-20, *"Knowing that you were not redeemed with corruptible things, like silver or gold, from your aimless conduct received by tradition from your fathers, but with the precious blood of Christ, as of a lamb without blemish and without spot. He indeed was foreordained before the foundation of the world, but was manifest in these last times for you."*

- 2 Corinthians 5:21, *"For He made Him who knew no sin to be sin for us, that we might become the righteousness of God in Him."*

- Hebrews 9:11-14, *"But Christ came as High Priest of the good things to come, with the greater and more perfect tabernacle not made with hands, that is, not of this creation. Not with the blood of goats and calves, but with His own blood He entered the Most Holy Place once for all, having obtained eternal redemption. For if the blood of bulls and goats and the ashes of a heifer, sprinkling the unclean, sanctifies for the purifying of the flesh, how much more shall the blood of Christ, who through the eternal Spirit offered Himself without spot to God, cleanse your conscience from dead works to serve the living God?"*

- The blood of different animals has different value. The blood of one man can't even pay the price for one man: Psalm 49:7-8, *"None of them can by any means redeem his brother, nor give to God a ransom for him—For the redemption of their souls is costly Only the blood of God could redeem all men!"*

- Revelation 5:9, *"And they sang a new song, saying:*

  *You are worthy to take the scroll, and to open its seals; For You were slain, and have redeemed us to God by Your blood. Out of every tribe and tongue and people and nation."'*

In these verses, we see how Jesus pursues us. He has done everything, removing every obstacle to bring us into relationship with Him.

His joy about His relationship with you empowers you to be like Him and live a powerful lifestyle of joy. You are now empowered to pursue others with His love bringing freedom and joy.

## I Care About His Need

This calls to mind another example of God erasing the mistakes of someone's past and preparing blessing for their future. This story begins when I was on a trip to the country of Columbia in South America. I was staying in the home of a precious older couple in a small town called Buga. This couple had three adult children; the family had close relationships. The husband and wife were consistently showing hospitality to their family and friends. Meal preparation was always in process, and half the neighborhood would show up when it was time to eat. I was impressed by the Columbian lifestyle that had such a high value for relationships and good food.

Early in my visit, I began to use my prophetic gift to encourage people in the house. After about a week, a steady stream of people continually came by the house to receive prayer and prophetic words. It was a very informal setting. Sitting at the dining room table with people, the older couples' bilingual daughter would translate my words from English to Spanish.

This older couple had a son who at the time was in his early thirties. I will refer to this man as Jorge to protect his privacy. Jorge was cheerful, curious and friendly. He had taken vacation and was staying at his parent's house during my visit. Jorge was watching me very closely, especially when I would prophesy over people. It turns out that he was deciding if I was safe enough to let me give him a prophetic word. He was being extra cautious, because he wanted to make sure I wouldn't use my prophetic gift to expose his past mistakes in front of his family.

With only about one day left in my two-week visit, Jorge came up to me and asked me to pray for him. Jorge and his bilingual sister, Linda, were sitting at the dining room table facing me. Almost immediately I heard the Lord speak this phrase to my heart: "Tell him I care about his need for companionship." Repeating this exact phrase to Jorge, he let out a very loud moan and began to weep.

After a few minutes, he took a deep breath and began to tell his story. Many of his large family were gathered around the table, listening to him. Jorge told us that a few years ago he had married a young woman, when they were both quite young. The wedding was in a Catholic church, and about a week after the wedding, his young wife abruptly and permanently left him. He was devastated, and eventually made an appointment with the priest at his church. Jorge explained to the priest that his wife had abandoned him. He did not want the marriage to end, but he had no way to contact his wife and didn't even know where she was. In an effort to honor the biblical sanctity of marriage, the priest explained to Jorge that there was no hope for him ever marrying again.

Jorge, in his early 20's, was profoundly disappointed and full of grief after listening to the priest. He decided God didn't care about his desire for companionship, so he would satisfy his own needs.

Jorge told us that he had spent the last few years being incredibly promiscuous. But this lifestyle was unfulfilling and he continued to be lonely. He was frustrated there was no way for him to be married, and he was deeply ashamed at his lifestyle and he felt hopeless. Jorge was naturally very pleasant, optimistic and sociable, but he hid his frustration and promiscuous lifestyle. He had not told anyone.

Sitting at his parent's dining room table, in front of his whole family, Jorge had a life-changing encounter with the goodness of God! Through my prophetic word, God had, in one sentence, pierced through all of Jorge's shame and given him hope. God had told Jorge, "I care about your need for companionship." Jorge was overwhelmed with the undeserved love of God, and God's love broke the power of his isolation. He was now free to be vulnerable and share his failures with his family and to ask God's forgiveness.

This event was the most dramatic and life-changing illustration of the Bible verse, *"the goodness of God leads you to repentance"* (Romans 2:4), I have ever witnessed. Jorge began to pour out his heart to his family about the promiscuity, the grief and shame. He now knew God loved him and cared about his desire for companionship. When God told Jorge He cared about his need for companionship, it had a double meaning. God wanted to give Jorge a loving wife, *and* He wanted to restore Jorge's relationship with Himself. God wanted to remove Jorge's sin and shame so their companionship could be restored.

So, I led Jorge in a prayer to receive God's forgiveness for his past behavior in front of his family. God forgave Jorge, and the family was moved with compassion and love for him. The shame and isolation vanished, and Jorge was given a new beginning.

Jorge was married a few years after this encounter with God. He now has a loving wife and two beautiful girls. Jorge is a great husband and father.

In the life of this man, God prepared a bright future, and His kindness spared him from the mistakes of his past (Psalm 139:5)! The hand of God's love upon his life is unmistakable. God's kindness and redeeming love is wonderful, deep and incomprehensible for this man, just as we read in Psalm 139:6. God's desire to know us and to bless should blow our minds!

Just as God pursues us, I was sent to Colombia and watched as Jesus pursued Jorge. Unimaginable joy filled not only my heart, but our Heavenly Father's heart as well! Another son had come home.

# CHAPTER 8

# The Lifestyle of Joy

I n order to know how to live a life of joy, we must first understand
the *heart* of the Apostle John. The Apostle John had a thorough
understanding of intimacy with the Lord. His epistles are mostly
about love.

**<u>Step One</u>: We Love Him Because He First Loved Us**

John was so transformed by God's love that it changed his identity. As a young disciple of Jesus, John was nicknamed a "son of
thunder" (Mark 3:17) for wanting to call down fire on an unre-
ceptive Samaritan village (Luke 9:54). As John was continually
exposed to the love of Christ, it transformed the way he viewed
himself and others. Several times in Scripture he describes himself
as "the disciple whom Jesus loved" (John 13:23 and John 21:7).
He was unashamed to put his head on Jesus' bosom (John 13:23).
Eight times in his epistles he refers to those in the churches in Asia
as "beloved."

As John focused on intimate fellowship with the Lord, he found
out it was integral to a lifestyle of joy. Once he had experienced this
lifestyle of joy, he wanted everyone to experience it:

*"That which we have seen and heard we declare to you, that you also may have fellowship with us; and truly our fellowship is with the Father and with His Son Jesus Christ. And these things we write to you that your joy may be full"* (1 John 1:3-5).

Since John became a master at receiving God's love, he is well equipped to instruct us in that same area. In John 4:19, he says,

*"We love Him because He first loved us."*

John *loved Jesus* because he learned to *receive love* from Jesus. It was the Lord's idea to love us long before we loved Him. God *"so loved* the world that he gave his only Son"* (John 3:16). With regard to love, the Lord is the initiator and we are the receivers. The only way we can effectively love God is to first receive his love. Receiving God's love is *step one*. We can't get anything right in our relationship with the Lord if we don't get *step one* right. Receiving God's love equips us to love Him back. Our ability to love God is completely determined by our receptivity to His love. It takes God to love God.

## Jesus Initiates Love

The dramatic story of a bride awakened by the bridegroom is depicted several times in Scripture. In Song of Solomon, which can be viewed as an allegory of our love relationship with Christ, the bride (Shulamite) is awakened by the bridegroom's kiss (Song of Songs 8:5 and 1:2). The entire drama of Christianity begins with Jesus loving us first. God, like the director of a drama, has cast us in His divine romance as the object of His love. And, He, as our Bridegroom, is the only one who can initiate it, first awakening us with a revelation of His love.

In the story *Sleeping Beauty*, the prince had to awaken the sleeping princess with his kiss. Just like this prince, Jesus awakens us out of our slumber by coming to us with a revelation of His love. Once we are awakened to His love, we are enabled to love Him back. We remain passive and paralyzed until our Jesus, as our Bridegroom, initiates love.

Jesus tells a parable describing virgins who are called to arise from their slumber to behold the coming bridegroom (Matthew 25:1-13). This parable, shows a passive and slumbering bride who must wake up to a revelation of God as a Bridegroom. Jesus is *initiating* love by *coming to them*, and their *response* to Him is to wake up.

Jesus initiates love towards you when He says in John 15:9, *"As the Father loved Me, I also have loved you; abide in My love."* This is an amazing statement. Jesus is saying that He loves you with the same intensity as He is loved by the Father. Then He tells you to live in a *constant state of being loved*. He tells you to cultivate a lifestyle where we are consistently receiving the same intensity of love that flows between members of the Godhead. Wow! This blows my mind! Can there be any better deal for the human race than to be invited to swim in the ocean of love that flows in the Godhead? If this were not possible as a lifestyle, Jesus wouldn't have told us to do it. Jesus never gives us a command without also giving us the ability to obey it.

Jesus has initiated love towards us, but only if we are *consistently receptive to His love will we be empowered to obey Him.* That is why Jesus doesn't even mention the word "commandments" until the next verse (John 15:10). Jesus knows we will fail any requirement to obey Him unless He first empowers to obey him with His love! The immensity of love Jesus gives us to empower our obedience is beyond human comprehension. He has to open our eyes to be able to believe it and receive it (Ephesians 3:14-19).

## Delighting to Do God's Will

Let's revisit the topic of Jesus being inspired by His Father's love and how He wants us to discover His lifestyle of joy too. Jesus says this: *"These things I have spoken to you, that My joy may remain in you, and that your joy may be full"* (John 15:11).

It is very important that we pay close attention to what Jesus teaches *immediately prior* to the above statement. Why? Because Jesus gave us the purpose of His teaching: He wants us to walk in the same lifestyle of joy that He does. If we are going to be successful in emulating Jesus' life of joy, we have to understand what He is saying prior to John 15:11.

In the Gospel of John, Jesus teaches us to live the same way He does. He unveils a pattern for how we can maintain joy while we walk in partnership with God. Since Jesus lived a life of joy, He wants us to live that way too. Because Jesus is filled with His father's love, it inspires Him to obey. As Jesus is filled with his Father's *delight, he delights to do his Father's will.*

What a gift from the Lord! He reveals, in practical terms, how to live a life of joy. Jesus mastered this joy-filled life. His motive in instructing us to live the way He does is so our *joy may be made full.* Let's continue taking a closer look at how our joy can be made full. The joy filled lifestyle is actually a cycle that begins with *receiving God's love* (step one).

## Step Two: Obedience Is Inspired by Love

The first thing Jesus teaches is that our obedience to God is the natural result of loving God. Jesus said, *"If anyone loves Me, he will keep My word"* (John 14:23). When our love relationship with the Lord is active and continuous, it inspires us to obey the Lord. If a person is having trouble obeying the Lord, they need to refuel their spirit's tank with the love of the Lord. Remember, we can't effectively love God unless we first receive love from Him (1 John 4:19). When the Lord's unconditional love fills our heart, it synchronizes our heart with the Lord. So, intimacy with the Lord transforms your will so you *want to* (instead of *have to*) obey Him.

The Lord's extravagant and undeserved love wins and softens our heart. If our heart was hard and self-willed, it becomes yielded and surrendered. Our desire to do the Lord's will arises from a heart *melted by love* rather than a heart *forced to obey*. This "new heart" is part of the glorious promise of the New Covenant. Jeremiah 31:31-34 discusses the coming promise. The Lord promises to *"write His law on our hearts"* so that we are changed from the inside-out. The law covenant gave us external obligations, but no power to obey them. Like Israel, we are doomed to keep breaking God's law as long as we have no direct access to His love.

But Jesus is determined to show us a better way! He wants us to have the same lifestyle with God that He has always enjoyed: a joyful partnership inspired by love, instead of grudging obedience inspired by fear.

Old Testament history demonstrates the failure of God's people to maintain obedience to God without direct access to His presence. In the Old Testament, obedience to God's law was mandatory, but only a few leaders had a personal relationship with God. God's people had good intentions to obey the Lord, but they ended up consistently disobeying. In 2 Corinthians chapter 3, Paul calls the Old Testament law *"the ministry of death"* and the *"ministry of condemnation"* (2 Corinthians 3:7,9). The law condemned people, because it gave them rules but didn't empower them to obey the rules. Under this covenant, God's people were caught in a hopeless cycle of good intentions, failure, and then repentance.

In 2 Corinthians 3:7-9 it tells us, *"But if the ministry of death, written and engraved on stones, was glorious, so that the children of Israel could not look steadily at the face of Moses because of the glory of his countenance, which glory was passing away, how will the ministry of the Spirit not be more glorious? For if the ministry of condemnation had glory, the ministry of righteousness exceeds much more in glory."*

Moses, on the other hand, had direct access to the presence of God. Intimate relationship with God transformed Moses so that his face shined. The face-to-face relationship Moses enjoyed with God infused him with divine power to obey the Lord. Moses had special access to God which was not available to the rest of Israel. Since Israel had no direct access to God, they couldn't maintain obedience. Without access to God's presence, no person can maintain obedience to God.

*"Nevertheless, when one turns to the Lord, the veil is taken away. Now the Lord is the Spirit; and where the Spirit of the Lord is, there is liberty. But we all, with unveiled face, beholding as in a mirror the glory of the Lord, are being transformed into the same image from glory to glory, just as by the Spirit of the Lord"* (2 Corinthians 3:16-18).

We are part of a superior covenant with God. Unlike people of God prior to Jesus' sacrifice, we have now been given direct access to God by the blood of Jesus. The ministry of the Spirit of God is more glorious, because now we can *all* look into God's face and be transformed! The law that condemned us has been disannulled, and we now are ruled by a new law: the *"law of liberty"* (2 Corinthians 3:17; Romans 8:2).

## My Challenge with Condemnation and Shame

When I was a younger Christian, I didn't understand this law of liberty. The statement by Jesus, *"If anyone loves Me, he will keep My word"* (John 14:23), caused me to struggle. I felt condemned by this verse. Having a sensitive heart, I sincerely wanted to be a lover of Jesus. But when I honestly assessed my life, I knew my obedience to the Lord was not flawless. Because I was not 100% obedient to every command of the Lord, I felt like an imposter, a phony. I thought my love for Jesus was genuine, but I had doubts because of this verse. *Maybe I really don't love Him, because my obedience to Him is not perfect.*

This kind of thinking caused me to run from the Lord in shame rather than *to* the Lord for encouragement. And as I ran from the Lord, I was forfeiting the very presence of God in my life that I needed to empower me to obey Him.

This is a perfect example of why the enemy is called *"the accuser of the brethren"* (Revelation 12:10). When sincere Christians are struggling in their obedience to God, the enemy tries to convince them they are hopeless hypocrites. He tries to paralyze them with shame to isolate them from intimacy with God. Remember Adam and Eve? Their shame after eating the forbidden fruit caused them to hide. The enemy tries to convince people that God is disgusted with them, and they are forever disqualified from being used by God.

He is a liar. I have come to realize that when sincere Christians disobey God it is more often due to weakness and immaturity than outright rebellion and defiance. The Lord is the Master at giving us victory in our struggles. He sees our *desire* to obey Him even if we sometimes lack the *ability* to obey Him.

Some would argue that emphasizing God's mercy gives people license to be sloppy in their obedience to Him. In my life, experiencing God's mercy has had the opposite effect. There have been times when I have been willing to obey the Lord, but I struggle in my ability to obey. At those times, I can either listen to the enemy's lies as the "accuser," or I can listen to the Lord, who is ever willing to be my Divine Encourager.

At times, I have been surprised by my own weakness and immaturity. But the Lord has been faithful to encourage me at the very time I needed (and still need) it. God strengthens my heart with His undeserved love, and it *restores my ability to obey Him.* The love and encouragement God gives me when I fail gives me the strength to keep following Him. The Lord sees my weakness and immaturity in certain areas, but He also sees my willing spirit. He knows how to help me mature in love with Him *so I can mature in obedience to Him.*

## Peter Is Re-fueled by the Lord's Love After He Fails

We all need to be reassured of the Lord's love when we fail. The amazing skill of Lord to encourage weak people who fail is best illustrated in the life of Peter. Impulsive and immature, Peter made a vow that he would not deny Jesus. Then, under intense pressure, Peter failed miserably. Peter was surprised by his own weakness, crushed by the shame of failing Jesus and disappointed by the crucifixion, so Peter gives up. He goes back to his previous career – fishing. Under the weight of his failure, he assumes the Lord is disgusted with him and has become disqualified from ever fulfilling his call to be an apostle. Peter lost strength to follow the Lord because he lost hope that the Lord still loved him.

But Jesus was not surprised by Peter's failure; He predicted it (Matthew 26:34). Before the crucifixion, Jesus told Peter in the garden, "The spirit indeed *is* willing, but the flesh *is* weak." (Matthew

26:41). Jesus saw Peter's weak flesh, *but He also saw his willing spirit.* Peter's encounter with Jesus at this point in his life raises a very important question: how does Jesus respond to genuine and sincere people like us, who sometimes fail Him because of weakness and immaturity? Or, put another way, *does the Lord's love for us fail when our obedience fails?*

The answer for Peter and for us is no! Jesus intervenes in Peter's life by showing up at the end of his fishing trip. The resurrected Jesus, Master of encouragement, appears on the beach (John 21). The disciples have just completed a whole night of unsuccessful fishing, and so Jesus supervises a successful catch right near the shore. Jesus loves them, and He has come to cook them breakfast. The main reason He is there, though, is to encourage Peter.

Jesus asks Peter if he loves Him. *"Do you love Me?"* This is a very difficult question for Peter, because he just failed to keep his vow to Jesus. Peter is ashamed, and he doesn't want to make another claim about himself that he can't back up. So sheepishly, Peter replies, *"Yes, Lord; you know that I love You"* (John 21:15). Jesus gets Peter to repeat that statement three times, effectively canceling Peter's three denials. Jesus is also breaking the shame off Peter and fully restoring him to ministry. Jesus tells him to *feed My sheep.*

Jesus wants Peter to make an accurate statement about his true identity. Peter views himself as a hopeless hypocrite, but Jesus sees the truth about who Peter is: a sincere lover of God. Peter is surprised by the weakness and immaturity he displayed by denying Jesus, and he assumes that his failure defines his identity. However, Jesus has a more accurate view of Peter's identity. Jesus knows Peter's love for Him is genuine even though he has failed. Jesus is telling Peter, *I see you are a genuine lover of God, now I want you to say it!* Jesus gets Peter to confess his accurate identity. A person's view of themselves matching how the Lord sees them is vital.

The Lord says something amazing to Peter before Peter's three denials. In Luke 22:31-32 Christ says, *"Simon, Simon! Indeed, Satan has asked for you, that he may sift you as wheat. But I have prayed for you, that your faith should not fail; and when you have returned to Me, strengthen your brethren."*

By all accounts, Peter's faith *did* fail. Jesus is telling Peter that He will remain *faithful to Peter even when Peter is not faithful to Him.* At the time Peter is displaying his worst behavior, he discovers the Lord's rock-solid faithfulness. Having made a fresh discovery of the undeserved mercy of the Lord, Peter is able to now "strengthen his brethren."

Peter's encounter shows that Jesus is incredibly merciful and encouraging to weak people who are trying to follow Him! When we are paralyzed by the shame of failing Him, Jesus comes to us to break the shame off of us. If we get mired in an attitude of shame, it will cause us to run away from Jesus at the very time we need His love to fuel our obedience.

## Jesus Purchased Our Access to God

That is why Jesus died for us. His death made it possible for us to enjoy forgiveness so we can maintain access to His presence. The Lord knows that His love inspires our obedience, so He purchased our access to God's presence to empower us to obey. Christ purchased an incredibly costly gift for us, which should never be taken for granted. Jesus knew we would be helpless to obey God unless we were inspired by His love. Remember, it was the Lord who said, *"If anyone loves Me, he will keep My word"* (John 14:23).

The lifestyle of joy begins with receiving God's love (1 John 4:19). Receiving God's love is step one. Then, God's love empowers us to love Him back. Now that we have power to love God, we are then inspired by God's love to obey Him. Our obedience is inspired by our intimate relationship with God. In this relationship, there is a reciprocal flow of love between us and God. God initiates love, we receive His love, and then love flows back and forth between us.

In the context of intimacy, our heart becomes synchronized with the Lord's heart. The strength we receive from the Lord's enjoyment of us (Nehemiah 8:10) empowers us to obey Him. The love and joy flowing from the Lord to us energizes our spirit. Our energized spirit, full of the Holy Spirit, becomes the primary influence upon our will. Now, we *want to* obey the Lord instead of *having to* obey Him.

We want to obey Him because our heart is melted and yielded to the One we love. We are delivered from being forced to do God's will in an effort to fulfill a mandatory requirement. Now, we are inspired to do God's will because we have been surprised by His extravagant and underserved love. We are delivered from striving to obey impersonal commands. Instead, we become passionately yielded to the One who has won our heart.

## <u>Step Three</u>: Jesus and the Father Make Their Home in Us

Being inspired by love to obey the Lord is only the beginning of this lifestyle of joy. The next thing the Lord promises us is this: *"If anyone loves Me, he will keep My word; and My Father will love him, and We will come to him and make Our home with him"* (John 14:23).

As we learn to receive the Lord's love and be inspired to obey Him, our life becomes a house the Godhead wants to permanently dwell in. Our lifestyle is like a welcome mat for the Lord. He wants to come and live in us. He desires to set up His home in us. He wants to abide there, not just visit once and a while.

The Lord expresses His desire to dwell with us throughout the Bible. In the beginning, God created Adam so He could commune with him in the garden, because God wanted to dwell with man. When the Lord called Moses to build a tabernacle in the wilderness, it was because He wanted to "dwell among" His redeemed people (Exodus 25:8). And Jesus came to earth as "Immanuel," meaning "God with us." The desire of God to dwell with man is best summed up in the book of Revelation:

*"And I heard a loud voice from heaven saying, 'Behold, the tabernacle of God is with men, and He will dwell with them, and they shall be His people. God Himself will be with them and be their God'"* (Revelation 21:3).

The message to the church of Laodicea in the book of Revelation shows us that Jesus wants to access to the door of our hearts so He can come in and dine with us (Revelation 3:20). He wants to live in our home so He can have intimate fellowship with us. In His message to the church at Laodicea, Jesus is seen knocking on the door, but their lukewarm hearts are restricting His access. The Lord rebukes them for their lack of passion for Him.

The message to us is clear. If we respond to the Lord's extravagant love with a love that is weak and passionless, it is insulting to the Lord. Since we are loved by the greatest lover in the universe, He expects us to love Him as passionately as He loves us.

Our lack of passion for Him is a symptom of our inability to accurately perceive His passion for us. So, God tells the Laodiceans to "anoint their eyes with eye salve, that they may see" (Revelation 3:18). Somehow, they have developed a problem with their ability to accurately see the Lord. Their inaccurate perception of the Lord has resulted in a lack of passion for Him, and so now the Lord is standing *outside their house*, knocking. Jesus wants them to correct their perception of Him so they can again see the intensity of His red-hot love for them and *make a home* for Him in their hearts.

We have to keep feeding our spirits on the Lord's love for us in order to maintain the love for Him that He deserves. If our perception of the Lord grows dim, we are left with a lukewarm heart. A lukewarm heart is not a place the Lord feels welcome. Jesus says this: *"As the Father loved Me, I also have loved you; abide in My love"* (John 15:9).

The intensity of the Father's love for Jesus is like the red-hot magma of a volcano. There cannot be a love more intense than this. Jesus tells us we are loved with the same intensity that the Father loved Him. This is incredibly good news!

Then, Jesus tells us to "abide" in His love. His intense love for us has made it possible for us to live with an intense love for Him. His desire is for a relationship with us where there is a reciprocal flow of intense love. It is possible to live this way, because Jesus tells us to abide in His love.

So, Jesus wants to dwell in a heart and a house with a fire. His love for us enflames our love for Him. He provides the fire, and we offer a place for it to continually burn. What a privilege we have to be empowered by His love to love Him. What an amazing gift it was when His death opened up direct access to His presence! The love we receive in His presence inspires us to follow and obey Him, and what an indescribable blessing it is to have Him set up His home in us!

## Step Four: Jesus Will Manifest Himself to Us

Here is the next step in the lifestyle of joy: the Lord promises to progressively reveal Himself to us. Jesus says:

*"He who has My commandments and keeps them, it is he who loves Me. And he who loves Me will be loved by My Father, and I will love him and manifest Myself to him"* (John 14:21).

The only way to really know someone is to spend time with them. So, as the Father and the Son are *"making their home with us"* (John 14:23), we are getting to know them. As we grow in intimacy with the Lord, He gives us a progressively more accurate revelation of Himself.

The word "manifest" in John 14:21 means to make known or to disclose. In this verse, Jesus is promising to make Himself known to us so we can *really* know Him. This is good news, because we cannot come to a complete or accurate knowledge of the Lord without His help. I have found the Lord is actually better than *I think* He is and better than *I feel* He is. The Lord is who *He says He is.* God's Word is my source to help me come to an accurate knowledge of Him. But I also need the Lord to *illuminate* His Word to me.

One of the functions of the Holy Spirit is to shine light on the very Word that He inspired. Jesus said the Holy Spirit will "guide you into all truth" (John 16:13). Jesus also said the Holy Spirit will *"take of Mine and declare it to you"* (John 16:15). The word "declare" in this verse means to disclose or make known, similar to the word "manifest" in John 14:21. The Holy Spirit shines light on Jesus so we can see Him in His full glory.

### Step Five: To Know Him Is to Love Him

The more the Lord discloses Himself to us, the more we are enabled to love Him.

Progressive love in a marriage is not stale; it is not based on yesterday.

## Jesus; The Shame-Breaker

Hebrews 12:1-2, *"Therefore, we also, since we are surrounded by so great a cloud of witnesses, let us lay aside every weight, and the sin which so easily ensnares us, and let us run with endurance the race that is set before us, looking unto Jesus, the author and finisher of our faith, who for the joy that was set before Him endured the cross, despising the shame, and has sat down at the right hand of the throne of God."*

## Despising the Shame

Jesus disregarded the shame, rejected the shame, ignored the shame, refused to receive the shame, refused to be defined by shame, and refused to believe that shame applied to Him.

Jesus remained completely convinced of His true dignity, even though the whole world was trying to impart shame to Him.

Humankind tried to dishonor the Son, yet He didn't receive it. Now, redeemed humans will honor the Son of God for eternity.

We crowned Him with a crown of thorns in an effort to dishonor Him, and now we cast our crowns before Him and will for all eternity honor and adore Him.

In taking our shame upon Himself, He refused to lose His essential dignity.

He bore our shame so He could restore our dignity. He rejected shame and focused on you as His source of joy to endure the cross. Now, you can also reject shame by focusing on His joy for you! This is how He has enabled you and I to walk free of shame.

He refused to be defined by our shame. At the very time He was enduring the attempt of humankind to massively shame Him, He intentionally chose to focus on you and I as the object of His delight!

This response to being dishonored is epic! Rather than becoming offended by being treated with such undeserved dishonor, He chooses to consider the ones who are dishonoring Him as the object of His delight!

This is why the "Lamb upon the Throne" is the One to whom all honor and adoration will be given for eternity.

*"Looking unto Jesus, the author and finisher of our faith"* (Hebrews 12:2).

For us to grow in faith (Jesus being the author and finisher of our faith) we need follow the pattern of our Savior.

Specifically, we are to focus on how He maintained His dignity in the face of dishonor and how He rejected the identity of shame that the world was trying to force on Him.

Although He did not deserve it, and He couldn't be forced to receive the world's shame, He voluntarily took our shame so He could give us His dignity.

Jesus wants you to reject shame as effectively as He did. You bear His nature, so shame no longer applies to you any more than it applies to Him.

Jesus also wants you to embrace His dignity as effectively as He did. Jesus identified Himself as the Father's beloved Son. You are just as much the "boy of His joy," and the "girl who makes Him twirl" as He is "the boy who brings His Father joy."

**My Testimony of God Removing My Shame**

I believe God wants to heal our hurting broken places; our broken places effect how we live our lives today. When we encounter a situation that pushes our buttons and we over react, this may be a sign of a broken place. Like a flashing red light, it's a sign that there

70

may be an area where God wants to bring the full exchange and manifestation of healing and wholeness for which Christ suffered.

During a time of inner healing while I was receiving prayer, I saw a picture of myself alone in my room at age of three. Afraid and alone, I feel spiritual darkness. An impenetrable bubble surrounds me, with the Lord on the outside.

The Lord snaps His fingers, and the bubble is gone. Then, He invites me up on His lap. He says, "I love the way I made you, and I am giving you a gift of faith."

## An Experience from When I Was Eight Years Old

Another instance floods my memory. I had defaced my sister's play kitchen refrigerator. Motivated by childlike irresponsibility and boredom, and perhaps some desire to be a pain in the rear, I drew an elaborate masterpiece on the refrigerator with crayons. Tired of my massively stressed-out mom during the move to a new city, I found mischief. After being sent to my room, I lay down on my bed to see what certain punishment awaited.

Dad comes in my bedroom and jumps on top of me, and the rage and anger are so intimidating. I make an internal decision that there is "something deeply wrong with me." I agree with a spirit of shame.

In a separate prayer time, I again see myself on my bed during this event, but this time is different. The Lord positions Himself between me and my dad. He absorbs the shame that was streaming to me from my father. Jesus fully absorbs the anger, the manipulation and the intimidation.

Right there He cancels the power of the shame, the manipulation and the intimidation – the illegitimate method my dad used to get me to behave better.

Jesus removed the root of perfectionism, performance-based approval and physical manifestations; He removed the heavy feelings and pressure those bring.

Jesus is GOOD at removing shame from me and helping me to feel His delight for me.

## Jesus Has Removed ALL of Our Shame

- Jesus defeated shame on the way to the cross by refusing to receive it. He rejected shame and focused on us as His delight.

- Jesus defeated shame on the cross by voluntarily taking our shame so He could give us His dignity. When we come to Christ, He removes our shame and gives us His dignity (prodigal son story). He does this to all "lost sons," because we are the object of the Father's joy.

- Jesus is still involved in removing shame from us and expressing His joy for us!

- The victory He accomplished for us He is now applying to us!

- We encounter His personalized, Great Physician skill as He takes us to the place and time where our heart was broken.

- He heals our broken heart.

- He absorbs the damage our hearts experienced from the failures, mistreatment and sinful actions of people.

- He absorbs the cruelty, the sin and the shame that people intended for us to absorb when they mistreated us.

- He enables us to forgive thoroughly from the heart, which is more effective than just general forgiveness in an effort to apply a biblical principle. He helps us to forgive thoroughly and specifically.

- He helps us to cancel wrong beliefs about ourselves and about God that keep us entangled in an inferior lifestyle.

- He applies the benefits of His atoning work in a way we don't know how to apply ourselves.

- He is our Great Physician!

Why did He do all of this? Jesus did it in order to bring us into freedom and give us the power to live a lifestyle of joy.

Just as John was so transformed by God's love, so much that it changed his identity, God has done the same for you and me. As we are continually exposed to the love of Christ, it transforms the way we view ourselves and others.

We are now empowered as sons and daughters to live a joy-filled life going into the world and sharing God's joy with others. We are God's creative partners as we share, they, too, will come to know the overwhelming goodness and love of God.

# CHAPTER 9

# You are God's Creative Partner

I n the last chapter, we looked at the expression of mutual delight in the Godhead as they went about the work of creation. As we've previously discussed, the creative partnership between the Father and His Son was more like a party than a job site. The father *daily* delighted in His Son and Jesus was *always* rejoicing. With so much joy and rejoicing going on, it is amazing anything got accomplished. What appears to be a scene of light-hearted fun and frivolity is actually a place of magnificent accomplishment.

## Joy and Divine Design

Consider the awesome wonder of creation. The beauty and the design of heaven and earth is a marvel of creative genius. Artists are inspired by creation's beauty, and scientists are motivated by discovery of nature's design. Creation obviously was not something haphazardly slapped together by a couple of frivolous partners. How did Father and Son create such a masterpiece and still maintain an atmosphere of delight in their relationship?

The Father and Son are an example to us. They demonstrate that in a relationship, it is possible to have both great enjoyment *and* amazing accomplishment. In fact, the love and intimacy that existed between Father and Son was necessary for the Father to progressively disclose his creative design to His Son. Full disclosure of the Father's dream was possible because Jesus was so close to His Dad. Jesus instinctively knew how to carry out His Father's creative design because He was inspired by His Father's love and delight.

In Psalm 40:8, Jesus said, *"I delight to do Your will, O my God, And Your law is within my heart."* The Hebrew word for "law" in that verse means "divine instruction." Jesus was simultaneously filled with divine delight and divine instruction to carry out His Father's will. Joy filled Jesus' emotions at the same time that divine knowledge filled His mind. The Father's joy empowered Him and the disclosure of the Father's plan equipped Him to carry out His Father's will.

We see joy and creative partnership between the Father and His Son also pictured in Hebrews 1:8-10. The Father is speaking to the Son: "But to the Son *He says: 'Your throne, O God, is forever and ever; A scepter of righteousness is the scepter of Your kingdom. You have loved righteousness and hated lawlessness; Therefore God, Your God, has anointed You with the oil of gladness more than Your companions.' And: 'You, LORD, in the beginning laid the foundation of the earth, And the heavens are the work of Your hands.'"*

These verses describe the heart of Jesus. He *loved righteousness* is a phrase that describes a Son whose heart is fully synchronized with His Father's heart. Think about this: He was full of more joy and gladness than any person who has ever lived. Jesus was full of joy, full of love for His Father's will, and therefore full of ability to be His Father's creative partner (vs.10).

**You Are Invited to Be God's Creative Partner**

Without true intimacy, a person can never really discover the dreams and desires of their partner. This is the relationship God is calling you to. He birthed you into His Kingdom because He wanted you to be His child. Everything He enjoys with Jesus He wants to enjoy with you. He wants you to be so close to Him that your heart and His heart become one. You get to be the object of His joy as He progressively discloses His dreams to you.

He wants you to feel His delight as your motive to create with Him. He wants His joy to be your strength. You get to playfully celebrate relationship with Him while He shares His power to create with you. An invitation is waiting; He has invited you to be His creative partner, in which your agreement with His will in heaven brings His will into reality on earth.

**Abraham Was God's Creative Partner**

We can see God's desire for creative partnership with man as we consider His interaction with notable Bible characters.

The Lord sovereignly called Abraham into covenant with Himself. God promised Abraham that through him all the nations of the earth would be blessed. But Abraham was called to more than to only bless nations. God invited Abraham to be His creative partner.

In the New Testament, Abraham is called the *"friend of God"* (James 2:23). Friendship with God transformed Abraham; he became unwilling to settle for anything less in life than what God was capable of building. Friendship *with* God removes a person's desire to build something *without* God. God's plans are more majestic than man's plans, and so a friend of God becomes inspired by God's dreams. Abraham realized that God's dream was bigger and more wonderful than anything he could implement on his own. He was willing to leave all that was familiar on a quest for a city that was not built by man's plans, agendas or ambition. Abraham *"waited for the city which has foundations, whose builder and maker is God"* (Hebrews 11:10).

As God's creative partner, Abraham's role seems passive, but it really wasn't. As the *"father of faith,"* Abraham's role in his partnership with God was to believe God, be patient and let God do the work.

Like Abraham, God calls *you* His friend. In John 15:13-15, Jesus calls us His friends three times! *"No longer do I call you servants, for a servant does not know what his master is doing; but I have called you friends, for all things that I heard from My Father I have made known to you"* (John 15:15).

A friend is not just a *worker for God*; he is a *partner with God*. A friend of God knows what God is doing. Jesus does not leave us ignorant, because He is disclosing His plans to us. The disclosure of God's plans in the context of intimacy is exactly like the relationship Jesus has always enjoyed with His Father (Proverbs 8:29-31). Jesus gets close to His Dad, and His Dad shows him *really* amazing stuff. We get close to Jesus, and reveals to us what His Father has shown Him! We get to be God's friends!

**Moses Was God's Creative Partner**

Moses was given divine instruction to build the tabernacle and to lead Israel while he was enjoying face-to-face relationship with God (Exodus 25-31; Exodus 33:11). The glory of God's face transformed the face of Moses (Exodus 34:29-35; 2 Corinthians 3:2).

Moses was completely dependent on God to lead him. But, to Moses, relationship with God was as important as leadership from God. In Exodus 33:13, He asks God to *"show me your way, that I may know you."* In this verse, Moses is asking God to guide his life, but his goal is to *know the Lord.*

*"'Now therefore, I pray, if I have found grace in Your sight, show me now Your way, that I may know You and that I may find grace in Your sight. And consider that this nation is Your people.'* And He said, *'My Presence will go with you, and I will give you rest.'* Then he said to Him, *'If Your Presence does not go with us, do not bring us up from here'"* (Exodus 33:13-15).

When Moses asks God to *"show me your way, that I may know you,"* God's response to Moses is, *"My presence will go with you."* This response from God shows the nature of Moses' relationship with God. God instructed Moses, but the relationship was not formal or impersonal, like a professor instructing a student. God did not interact with Moses strictly for the purpose of dispensing information or issuing a directive. Moses and God were friends!

*"So the LORD spoke to Moses face to face, as a man speaks to his friend"* (Exodus 33:11).

Moses placed such value on this life-giving, first-hand relationship with the Lord that he had no interest in leading Israel if he had to do it without God's presence. Once Moses experienced face-to-face relationship with God, he would not live without it.

So, Moses, like Jesus, experienced delight coming from God's face and instruction coming from God's heart. Moses simultaneously experienced the glory of God's joy and the genius of God's plan. God loves to reveal His divine design to build and to lead, but He fuels our heart with His joy to accomplish the task.

### David Was God's Creative Partner

Like Moses, David had the experience of loving to see God's face, and then receiving instruction in the context of intimacy. David was anointed by Samuel to be king, and then he encountered a whole host of character-building trials. Running from Saul, fighting battles and facing pressure on every side, David had only one place he could find relief. The pain of life drove him into God's presence. David discovered that being with God was his number-one desire.

In Psalm 27:4, David says: *"One thing I have desired of the LORD, that will I seek: That I may dwell in the house of the LORD all the days of my life, to behold the beauty of the LORD, and to inquire in His temple."*

With so much conflict in David's life, he might have sought God to solve his problems or provide him with war strategies. But this wasn't his primary goal. David says his one desire is to behold God's beauty. David had no complicated motive. He was going to God for the simple pleasure of face-to-face intimacy. David was a man after God's own heart, and so being with God delighted both the heart of David and the heart of the Lord. The pleasure of this mutually delightful relationship with God was David's relief from the pain of life.

As David enjoyed God, he was hidden from trouble (Psalm 27:5). The location of David's shelter with God is notable. David's shelter was not in a bunker in the valley, it was located "high upon a rock." David's primary goal was to behold God's beauty, but in the process of pursuing intimacy with God, David got elevated to a higher position. The *throne room* where he enjoyed God was also the *war room where he got instruction from God.* First it was enjoyment, and then it was instruction.

This is identical to the pattern of how Jesus interacts with His Father in Proverbs 8:29-31. Jesus is enjoyed by His Father, and then He creates with His Father. David first beholds God's beauty, and then he *"inquires in His temple"* (Psalm 27:4). To inquire means to ask or to seek. David was getting instruction from God in the context of intimacy with God. As David was elevated with God, he was able to view the battle from a higher perspective:

*"And now my head shall be lifted up above my enemies all around me"* (Psalm 27:6).

So, like Jesus, David is the Lord's intimate companion and his creative partner. David is a warrior, so as he is being enjoyed by God, he gains instruction from God necessary to be victorious in battle.

## Paul Was God's Creative Partner

Paul says he is "wise master builder" of the church, according to the grace God gives him (1 Corinthians 3:10). The term "wise master builder" reminds me of the word Jesus uses to describe Himself during His partnership with the Father in the process of creation: "Master Craftsman" (Proverbs 8:30). Both Jesus and Paul are describing a creative partnership with God in which the creative product is a master work of art.

When God creates with us, the end result is so beautiful, functional and stable that it is displays His creative genius. The amazing thing is, God invites us into intimacy with Him so that He can unfold His creative plans to us. Paul was invited into intimacy with God, but it took time for God to change Paul's priorities.

Paul was so capable that it was not easy for him to depend on God. Paul had a long list of human qualifications. Early in his life, his impressive resume convinced him he could build the Kingdom in his own ability. Paul was so full of zeal and human ability that God had to wean him off dependence upon his own strength. Paul lists all his impressive human qualifications in Philippians 3:2-6, and then he concludes,

*"But what things were gain to me, these I have counted loss for Christ. Yet indeed I also count all things loss for the excellence of the knowledge of Christ Jesus my Lord, for whom I have suffered the loss of all things, and count them as rubbish, that I may gain Christ"* (Philippians 3:7-8).

Paul, the super-achiever, tossed all his achievements in the trash, so that he "might know" Christ (Philippians 3:10). The desire to intimately know Christ is something we expect from David the worshipper or John the Apostle (the lover of Jesus). But the fact that Paul's primary goal became knowing Christ is a human transformation of epic proportions!

Every person who encounters God in a genuinely intimate relationship becomes inspired to give up every inferior pursuit. Once Abraham became God's friend, he wouldn't try to build a city without God. Once Moses became God's friend, he was given instructions to lead Israel, and he wouldn't go anywhere without God. Once David became God's friend, he had one desire: to behold God's beauty. Once Paul experienced an intimate relationship with God, everything else became rubbish so that he could know God.

Once a person has experienced intimacy with God, it becomes their primary goal. And that is true for every person, regardless of their temperament or drive to achieve. Paul, the achiever, completely revised his agenda so his goal to know Christ became first priority. Knowing Christ then became the source of Paul's ability to be a wise master builder.

## We Can Become God's Creative Partners

One workday at about 4:00 p.m., I walked into a Mexican restaurant for an inspection. A few minutes after I began my inspection, the manager, named Maria, introduced herself to me. Maria walked with me as I conducted the inspection. There were no customers for the duration of my inspection. I asked Maria, "How is business at your restaurant?" She told me, "Business has been very slow."

As the inspection progressed, I felt the Lord whisper to me, "Tell Maria I love her." I took note of what the Lord had told me, and was intending to give Maria this message after completing the inspection. Interestingly, though, I heard the Lord repeat this phrase six more times in the next 30 minutes: "Tell Maria I love her." It was very unusual for the Lord to repeat an identical phrase to me; He knew I intended to give Maria His message after the first time He told me. But in this case, He was making it abundantly clear how emphatically He wanted to communicate this to her.

By this time in my life and ministry, I was confident in my ability to hear from the Lord. Usually, the Lord gives me a much more detailed prophetic word that is so uniquely personal it gets someone's attention. But the word to Maria was simply, "Tell her I love her." I thought to myself, "This prophetic word doesn't feel that powerful; it is not very specific or personal. This word is so general, I could give this to anyone." Frankly, I was unimpressed with the content of this word, even though it was clear to me the Lord was determined for me to tell her.

After the inspection ended, I sat down at a dining room table with Maria. I told her the Lord had persistently repeated this phrase seven times to me: "Tell Maria I love her." Maria sat there listening to me without any conspicuous reaction. She was silent for about 20 seconds, which prompted me to ask her, "What are you thinking?"

She said, "I am stunned by what you just said." She told me she had been overwhelmed and discouraged that whole day. Just a half hour before I arrived for the inspection, she was in her office with the door closed, distraught and crying. She told me she had become a Christian about a year before and her husband was not pleased with her decision. Her husband initiated a divorce and abruptly left her without any financial support. She had become the sole bread-winner for her family. Her round-trip travel to and from work was about an hour and 45 minutes each day. On the job, she was working about 50 hours a week, and had almost no time with her children.

She told me she was worried about her teenage son, because he was using drugs and hanging out with the wrong people. She was feeling guilty for being absent from her children, and she felt like she was not a good mother. On this particular day, all her troubles were just too overwhelming, so she rushed into her office to be alone and cry. While she was crying, she cried out to the Lord in prayer. She told the Lord about her grief, her guilt and her fear. Then, she prayed a very specific prayer to the Lord. She said, "Lord, I just need to know for sure that You love me."

After hearing her story, I was stunned! I now realized why the Lord was so emphatic and persistent with me that I *tell Maria I love her*. Now, I realized why the Lord kept repeating that same phrase to me. The Lord wanted me to use the exact wording Maria had prayed for! This wording had first seemed to me like too general of a prophetic word, but it turned out to be the exact wording the Lord wanted her to hear!

Maria and I sat there and marveled at the Lord's faithfulness and perfect timing! The Lord had miraculously confirmed His love for her in the way she had asked Him to. The Lord's timing was perfect for both of us. His timing was perfect for Maria, because He encouraged her at the time of her greatest need. His timing was perfect for me, as he was sovereignly guiding the normal activity of my life so I could be a miraculous messenger of His love to Maria.

I never get tired of being one of God's creative partners through these prophetic adventures. God, in His infinite goodness, uses the mundane in my life as a backdrop for the miraculous! God's faithfulness in transforming me by His love has resulted in me becoming an expression of His transforming love to other people. Because God helped me discover "I am the boy who brings Him joy," I have been empowered me to express His joy for people. God expresses Himself through me because of what I have become, not because I am trying harder to love people.

It is a priceless privilege for us to walk with the Lord and be a first-hand participant in His divine drama to love people. He is so good at loving, encouraging, comforting and freeing people. And what an honor it is that He has invited us to join Him in this quest of partnership as we become a healthy family in the earth

# CHAPTER 10

# The Church Becoming a Healthy Family

As we become healthy sons and daughters, empowered by the Lord's joy for us, we are enabled to become the healthy, redeemed family the Lord has always dreamed of. The church, as the corporate expression of mature children, reflects the health of the Godhead, and thereby credibly reveals the plan of God to the world (John 17:21-23).

Jesus has invested all of Himself in bringing to birth His church. The purpose of his incarnation as the God-man was to reveal God to man and to reconcile man to God. His atoning work brought about the birth of his church. In His prayer to the Father just prior to the cross, Jesus places the highest priority on the His church becoming a healthy family. Jesus prays that the church will become an accurate and authentic reflection of Godhead as a healthy family. The vibrantly healthy interpersonal relationship between God the Father and God the Son has become the pattern for God's redeemed family, the church.

God's primary intent for His church is for it to be an expression of healthy family. However, local churches in modern times are not always expressions of healthy family as their primary purpose. Churches can be primarily institutions, businesses or religious ceremonies. The church becoming healthy family needs to be as much a priority for church leaders as it is to the Lord Himself.

The Godhead is heaven's prototype family. It provides mankind with the perfect pattern for relational health in God's redeemed family. The relationship between Jesus and His Father is the template for how a healthy multigenerational church should operate.

The Godhead is one God manifested in three persons. The main reason God revealed Himself to us in the form of three persons is to show us His high priority for family. The way members of the Godhead interact with each other is God's demonstration of healthy family to us.

In John 17, when Jesus gives his church "glory to become one" (John 17:22), He is empowering his redeemed family on earth to become just like heaven's healthy family, the Godhead. God's redeemed family on earth becoming an accurate corporate expression of God is God's plan for revealing Himself to the world.

Throughout history God has been progressively revealing Himself to mankind, but the most accurate revelation of God to man is Christ Himself.

*"The Son is the dazzling radiance of God's splendor, the exact expression of God's true nature—his mirror image!"* (Hebrews 1:3 TPT)

So, God, in the form of a man, is the perfect expression of God to man! Since Jesus is a flawless expression of God to man, if the world was able to accurately see Jesus, then God's goal of revealing Himself to the world would be accomplished. Following this logic, Jesus could have easily prayed something like this in John 17, "Father,

I have revealed You on earth, so I pray that You will help the world to see Me so they will know You sent Me."

Amazing as it is, Jesus is not asking the Father to help the world to see the revelation of God through the person of Jesus. Instead, Jesus asked the Father to help the world see the revelation of God through the mature church. Jesus is confident the mature church becoming healthy family will provide proof to the world that God sent His Son to redeem us and restore relationship with us.

The church becoming like the Godhead will be the credible source that convinces the world to wake up to the eternal plan of God. The key to reaching the world is the life, maturity, unity and love of the disciples.

The world will only be reached when the disciples come into the fullness of Christ and in unity of the faith (Ephesians 4:13). This is what consumes the heart of Jesus as He prays for them before the cross.

Twice in John 17:21-23 Jesus prays *"that the world may know"*:

*"...that they all may be one, as You, Father, are in Me, and I in You; that they also may be one in Us, <u>that the world may believe that You sent Me</u>." "And the glory which You gave Me I have given them, that they may be one just as We are one: I in them, and You in Me; that they may be made perfect in one, and <u>that the world may know that You have sent Me...</u>"*

Jesus is staking the entire redemptive purpose of God – revealing Himself to man and inviting us into relationship – on His church becoming as glorious, mature and healthy as the Godhead. The church that has become "one, even as the Son and the Father are one" (John 17:21) is the church that will inspire the world to recognize

Jesus. Jesus considers the definitive evidence of the reality of God will be demonstrated to the world through the mature church.

## Characteristics of the Godhead as a Healthy Family: Father and Son's Joy for Each Other

During the process of creation, we discussed how joy was a focal point of the relationship between the Father and His Son. The Father delighted in the Son, and the Son experienced His Father's delight, and rejoiced. They celebrated their creative work. There was more joy than they could contain, so they created mankind so we could all experience this joy with them. Their joy for each other inspired them to enlarge their family.

Jesus said, *"I was daily His delight, rejoicing always before Him, Rejoicing in His inhabited world, and my delight was with the sons of men"* (Proverbs 8:30-31).

Jesus was so full of the Father's delight that He directed His delight towards us ("the sons of men"). Mankind was created as the focal point of Christ's delight. Mankind was the fruit of joy in the Godhead.

## Epic Strategic Effectiveness

The Godhead is full of joy, but they are also effective at accomplishing their purpose. Creation is a dazzling display of their genius in art, engineering and biology. God's creation is both epically beautiful and functional.

God also shows creative genius in His redemptive plan for mankind. The Bible's central theme is the progressive unfolding of His redemptive plan. Each member of the Godhead plays an active role in both creation and redemption.

The Godhead functions as a remarkably joyful and relationally-healthy team. Their strategic effectiveness is an outflow of their relational health.

## Honor and Humility

### *The Father Honors His Son*

When Jesus became a man in the incarnation, it marked the beginning of the most significant thirty-three years in human history. The baby Jesus became a man, and at His baptism, the Father audibly expressed His joy for Jesus: "This is my beloved Son, in whom I am well pleased," (Matthew 3:17). At the commencement of Jesus's ministry, the Father affirmed Him for who He was. The Father's approval of Jesus was emphatically expressed before Jesus began His ministry.

While Jesus was on earth, the Father did not need to be in the spotlight; He was in a support role. This was Jesus's time to shine. Father God supported Jesus by honoring, affirming, guiding, and strengthening Him. There is a remarkable amount of humility and self-deference in the Godhead.

### *Jesus Honors His Father and the Holy Spirit*

Jesus is the most capable person who ever lived, but He chooses complete dependence on His Father for direction and on the Holy Spirit for empowerment. Jesus does nothing on His own initiative; He does only what the Father is saying and doing (John 5:19, 30 and 8:28).

Jesus doesn't need honor from men, but He honors His Father. One of the ways Jesus honors His Father is by doing His Father's will. (John 8:49-58).

As a child, Jesus grew and became "strong in spirit" (Luke 2:40). At His baptism, the Holy Spirit came to rest upon Jesus. Jesus relied on this ongoing source of empowerment from the Holy Spirit during His entire ministry (Luke 4:1, 4:14, 4:18).

Even though Jesus is the uniquely in the spotlight during His earthly ministry, He humbly postures Himself in complete dependence on the other two members of the Godhead. Rather than display His impressive competence apart from the Father and Holy Spirit, He displays complete dependence upon them.

*The Holy Spirit honors Jesus*

The Holy Spirit plays an integral role in selflessly supporting the Father and Son. In creation, He is hovering over the water, bringing order out of chaos, and preparing the way for God to speak (Gen. 1:2). During Jesus' ministry, Holy Spirit is serving, empowering and comforting the Son of God. Holy Spirit also raises Jesus from the dead (Romans 8:11).

The Godhead functions with amazing strategic effectiveness; they are each humble, interdependent and eager to support each other. They are selflessly integrated together to accomplish a common purpose.

**The Church as Healthy Family**

Jesus wants His redeemed family on earth to function with the same relational health and strategic effectiveness as the Godhead. The Godhead has shown the church how to be healthy family and now has supplied the grace necessary to become healthy family. When His church learns how to live just like the Godhead, it will be the answer to Jesus' prayer in John 17.

## The Beginning of My Journey to Experience Healthy Spiritual Family

When I was about 45 years old, I began to discover God enjoys me. This unfolding experience is the message of this book. As I discovered how much my Father God enjoyed me, I began to be transformed into a healthy son. The Lord re-parented me. What my parents were not able to give me as a son, the Lord Himself gave me.

My understanding of my own identity changed. As I was enabled to receive the Lord's love and joy for me, I began to see that He valued me for who I am and not for what I do. Beginning to relax, I let the Lord love me. What I did not know at the time was the Lord was also doing this in the lives of many Christian leaders in my region. Other leaders were also being transformed by the love of God as Father. As we were individually experiencing transformation, we were becoming healthy sons necessary to operate in healthy spiritual family.

About this same time in my life, my wife and I started a local church. As I was growing in my skill to pastor God's people, I longed for a gifted team of leaders to do ministry with. My wife and I had a call to pastor, but we didn't want to do it alone. We dreamed of working side by side with a complete, 5-fold ministry team. After pastoring this local church by ourselves for over a decade, we began to "bump into" gifted leaders in our region who also wanted to experience healthy 5-fold team ministry.

## Joining with Another Local Church

After about 12 years of pastoring along with my wife, suddenly I was meeting many like-minded Christian leaders in my region. We were motivated to learn how to work together rather than place all our effort into building our own local churches. We thought there might be a different way to do Kingdom. I developed friendships with a number of worship leaders in my region, and to my surprise, they began to lead worship about once a month in our church. So, our church, though relatively small, began to be an expression of friendship-based cooperation between leaders in a region.

I developed many new friendships with Christian leaders during this period. Among these new friendships were several pastors from a nearby church named Beach Chapel. Beach Chapel was part of the Wesleyan denomination pastored by a man named Larry, who had spent his earlier years pastoring in a Calvary Chapel church. The Wesleyan denomination had invited Larry to become the pastor at Beach Chapel, even though Larry was different in his church culture and some of his theology. Beach Chapel was a relatively conservative church with a systematic teaching emphasis.

Larry decided to attend a Randy Clark conference, and during the conference, he went forward to receive an impartation. Larry began to move in gifts of healing, and with great enthusiasm, introduced his new gifting to his local church. The congregation at Beach Chapel was less enthusiastic than Larry about his gift of healing. Sadly, about a third of his congregation left the church, and about another third was cautious and unsure. But Larry maintained both his courage and enthusiasm. After discovering God still heals people today, he wasn't about to change his mind, even if it meant losing church members or close Christian ministry friends.

Larry was in the process of turning the leadership of Beach Chapel to the next generation. The two younger pastors, Micah and Bourne, were unsure about this abrupt change in Larry. This led to an exciting and somewhat difficult journey for the trio of leaders at Beach Chapel. They decided to embrace the gifts of the Holy Spirit and learn a whole new way of leading the church.

The Beach Chapel leaders were humble and hospitable. They began to hold weekly evening meetings with an emphasis on worship and exploring the gifts. This meeting became a connection point of new relationships across the body of Christ. They had never pastored a spirit-filled church before, so Larry, Micah and Bourne were willing to learn from spirit-filled pastors in the region.

At this same time, my wife Sandy and I began to develop a deep and lasting friendship with the Beach Chapel pastors. We loved their beautiful hearts and kindred spirits. We began to feel the Lord's prompting to join the two churches together. After 14 years of senior pastoring and several years of praying together and planning, on Easter Sunday of 2017, the two churches became one.

## Joining of Two Churches and Two Generations

The merge of our two churches began our exploration of the joining of two generations. We felt God was challenging us and empowering us as a church to become a radically healthy, multi-generational family. Pastors Micah and Bourne are about 20 years younger than Sandy and I. The older generation needed to learn how to support the younger generation by giving them plenty of love, prayer and room to lead.

The Lord prompted all of us to explore church as an expression of healthy family. The Lord spoke to pastor Micah and I separately and told us we were on an "expedition" like Lewis and Clark. He wanted us to fearlessly explore new territory, and then open up a pathway for succeeding generations. We discovered the younger generation benefits by honoring the older generation and receiving their wisdom. The wisdom of the older leaders would only be valued by the younger leaders if they received loving support rather than controlling advice. The Lord prompted Sandy and I to back off and let the younger pastors lead.

The Lord helped us do the "multigenerational dance" without stepping on each other's toes. Navigating a generational transition in a local church is often not done well. The older leaders often leave the local church completely, removing all their influence and wisdom. Or the older leaders may stay at the local church, exerting their influence in a way the younger leaders don't feel the freedom and support to lead.

God wants His redeemed family on earth (the church) to be as healthy as the Godhead. He wants blessing and spiritual legacy to expand in successive generations. He is poised to empower us with a remarkable level of grace for healthy family. He is willing to help multiple generations in the church interact with humility, mutual honor, a high level of joy and strategic effectiveness.

## Key Characteristics of a Healthy Church Family

As leaders, we discovered some very practical aspects of the church as healthy family in our interpersonal relationships. God wanted us to live together with maximum honesty, authenticity, vulnerability, humility and joy. He challenged us to build a culture of healthy local church by practicing the values of His Kingdom culture ourselves – in our own families and homes. If the leaders in a church live a lifestyle that reflects the characteristics of the Godhead, then the whole church community is able to follow this example.

The Lord wants His leaders to practice healthy relationships so we can lead by example.

Healthy covenant relationships among church leaders begins with excellent communication. The Lord doesn't want us to hide from one another. He doesn't want us to avoid conflicts. His way to navigate conflict will increase our understanding and our connection with the other person, not cause a rift. Learning to walk together in true love and unity is an important part of our calling. Becoming strategically effective in our calling requires us to become healthy family.

Leaders tend to be gifted and ambitious people. But learning to work together as a team is how we discover true humility. The Lord doesn't throw a bunch of gifted leaders together just to change the world or accomplish a task. He wants us to become family. He wants us to pray for one another and contribute to each other's success. As iron sharpens iron, He knows we will become more selfless, and free of selfish ambition. He wants us to value each other's different perspectives. He also wants our love for one another to become so strong that our love becomes the strength of our covenant. We can seek to establish covenant with one another based solely on biblical principal, but the strongest covenant bond is based on love.

The Lord desires unity; He doesn't want us to be separated from one another because we have built walls of self-protection. Honesty requires courage, and we have to be convinced we will not be punished for our honesty. We can learn to be boldly, courageously vulnerable with each other. He wants us to be willing to show weakness with one another and be honest about our frustrations. He knows it's important for us to be able to admit when we are offended. When we are vulnerable, it should increase peoples love for you and inspire them to pray for you.

Once you have experienced the dynamics of a healthy team, you won't live any other way. It is simply a superior way of living! You become endeared to members of your leadership team because of their vulnerability toward you. Because of your prayers for them, you begin to see fellow church leaders becoming strong where they once were weak. The whole team begins to experience much joy in the process of fulfilling God's purpose in your lives together. Each person learns to follow the Lord together as you depend on the Lord to initiate among you what He is doing. Greater strategic effectiveness in your corporate calling as a church starts to manifest. You learn how to become more fruitful in God's Kingdom with less striving (John 15:5-8). You all learn together how to bear the light yoke (Matthew 11:28-30). Each person develops a lifestyle that draws strength from your connection to one another (Ephesians 4:15-17).

## Stumbling Into 5-fold Friendships

Some years ago, I began attending some regional 24-hour worship events. These 24-hour worship sessions were being held in different church sanctuaries around our county. The man coordinating them was inspired by the Lord to invite worship leaders from local churches to take turns leading worship for 24 hours. These worship sessions continued over a period of about two years and were conducted in 24 different church sanctuaries, representing all the different cities within our county.

To prepare for each session, they would relocate all the chairs in the sanctuary to the perimeter walls, leaving a large open space in the center. The rotating worship teams would set up in the middle of the room in a small circle, facing inward (towards one another). People from all churches were invited to participate in worship, with the focus being to minister directly to God rather than the more familiar habit of worshipping in preparation for a church service.

This sustained worship, with a focus on ministering to the Lord, was a prophetic act, reconsecrating a region to the Lord. It was a way of rededicating a region to the Lord by expressing a desire to place a priority on God's presence. This prophetic act also was a way acknowledging the Lord's church in our region was bigger and more interconnected than a bunch of isolated local churches. It demonstrated our desire to cooperate together, even if we didn't fully know how to live this way yet.

God responded by pouring out His grace for His worshipping church in a region to begin to form new friendships with one another. These new connections were based on a common desire for God's presence rather than our geographical proximity or local church affiliation.

This new experience was fun and exciting for me. I discovered a whole new group of precious friends. It felt like I was being given the privilege of experiencing an expanded regional church family. Before this time, my wife and I had been faithful as local church pastors, but we found ourselves unintentionally isolated from the rest of the body of Christ in our region. Pastors were fully focused on their own local churches, so there wasn't much effort extended to form deep, authentic relationships with church leaders outside our own four walls.

But this all changed in a matter of months for me. Many of the church leaders I met were tired of expending all their energy building their local church; they, too, were hungry for meaningful connections with other leaders. We wanted to find value in one another and contribute to each other's success in a way described by Paul in Philippians 2:3-4 (TPT):

*"Don't allow self-promotion to hide in your hearts, but in authentic humility put others first and view others as more important than yourselves. Abandon every display of selfishness. Possess a greater concern for what matters to others instead of your own interests."*

I discovered I was blessed by paying attention to "divine connections." There were certain people among my new-found friends who I felt especially inspired to build friendships with. Two of my closest friends became ministry partners during this time period: Mike Hubbard and Jamie Weston. We kind of unintentionally stumbled into one another in a way that was deeply enjoyable, and then it became strategic. As we built friendships, our love and honor for on another increased. As our love increased, so did our desire to contribute to the success of each other. Over the years, we discovered we can relax, humbly defer to one another and selflessly contribute to each other's success.

Mike, Jamie and I began to travel regularly together, both nationally and internationally. We formed a friendship-based informal ministry partnership. As we practiced this lifestyle with each other, we began to experience a powerful synergism in our friendship and in our public collaborative ministry together.

Without competing for ministry platform, we often experienced the Holy Spirit seamlessly integrate our public ministry in real time. The Lord was empowering us together in a way that made us more effective with less effort. Rather than "chomping at the bit" for our ministry partners to finish, hoping for our turn to minister, we were inspired and enhanced by what the others were saying. We discovered the joy of following the Lord together as we became increasingly comfortable with Spirit-led flexibility, enabling us to become less reliant on a rigidly structured pre-plan.

People would regularly comment on "how well we flowed together" as a team. We realized an important part of what God wanted to impart through us was not just our personal revelation, but our collective unity. He was using leaders who put an emphasis on their relationship as friends. Then, I realized modeling and imparting unity is one of the key functions of 5-fold ministry as described in Ephesians chapter 4:11-13 (TPT):

*"And he has appointed some with grace to be apostles, and some with grace to be prophets, and some with grace to be evangelists, and some with grace to be pastors, and some with grace to be teachers. And their calling is to nurture and prepare all the holy believers to do their own works of ministry, and as they do this they will enlarge and build up the body of Christ. These grace ministries will function until we all attain oneness into the faith, until we all experience the fullness of what it means to know the Son of God, and finally we become one into a perfect man with the full dimensions of spiritual maturity and fully developed into the abundance of Christ."*

Five-fold ministry is called to work together to equip the church and to bring her to the fullest expression of unity and maturity. That means 5-fold ministry in a region needs to function together in unity and maturity, because we will have no power to impart something to the church that we ourselves are not living. God's answer to bringing the church to unity and maturity is 5-fold ministers expressing a lifestyle of unity and maturity. God has issued divine grace to His church to become healthy family just like the Godhead (John 17:21), and God has entrusted 5-fold ministry to become forerunners in the lifestyle of healthy family. Only then will we complete our mandate to bring the church to unity and maturity.

It is important for 5-fold ministry in a region to find and value one another. In Revelation chapters 2 and 3, the churches are identified by a geographical locality, not an individual local church.

It is also important for 5-fold ministry called to the same geographical region to walk in authentic, Christlike humility, inspired by selfless love for one another. The character qualities of humility and selfless love are uniquely foundational to the building of God's Kingdom, because this lifestyle unlocks corporate authority and synergism. It is especially important for apostles and prophets to learn to live this way together, since they compose the foundation of the household of God (Eph. 2:19-20).

Humility and selfless love are like strong steel rebar in a concrete foundation. Only then can the 5-fold ministers of the church in a region become covenant partners, correctly aligned in order to build together.

# CHAPTER 11

# God's Progressive Expression of Himself in Us

When we think about God's expression of Himself in us, at Christmas time, we think about the incarnation, don't we? At Christmas, we think about how God became a man to reveal Himself to us. And so, as I'm thinking about God revealing Himself to us, I feel God highlighting this for me: *"But that wasn't My end goal, Bill. My end goal wasn't to reveal Myself to you. It was to reveal myself in you and through you. That's My end goal."* Christ revealed at Christmas as a baby was just the very beginning of a progressive expression of Himself to and in us.

## You Are Significant

This reminds me of another Christmas season. I was visiting Reno, Nevada, one very cold week in December. When I entered a restaurant to conduct an inspection, I met a young, Hispanic man who told me he had been working as the manager for only a few days. This man was thin with arms covered in tattoos. He had some minor swelling on the left side of his face, and he kept reaching up to touch this area as if he was in pain. He was acting nervous about the inspection, and he told me he was very open to learning anything I could teach him. As he accompanied me on the inspection, he told me he was not very knowledgeable in his position as manager and felt insecure. Impressed by his vulnerability, I immediately felt a wave of the Lord's compassion for him.

He told me he'd had a rough life; he had spent several years in jail and had only been out of jail for a few months. I asked him about the swelling on his jaw area, and he told me he had an infection under his molar, and it was very painful. He didn't want to tell his boss about the tooth infection, because he had recently been hired and wasn't sure he had health insurance coverage yet. Not having the money to pay out of pocket for the dentist, he decided to endure the pain.

After completing the inspection, I asked him to sit with me at a table in the dining room. I told him I wasn't just a health inspector, but I was also a pastor. He was happy to hear that, and told me he had recently started reading the Bible when he was in jail.

I felt compassion for his physical pain. I told him a tooth infection like his can be serious and he shouldn't wait to see the dentist. I told him I would like to pray for his tooth. Reaching out, I gently touched the side of his face and prayed healing for his tooth infection. I added, "See a dentist promptly if the pain continues."

I could see the pain in his eyes as he looked at me. It was more than the physical pain of the toothache; it was also the cumulative pain of a difficult life. I told him I was feeling the heart of a father for him, and said, "I can feel your importance to the Lord as a son." I asked if it was alright if I encouraged him and prayed for him. He was surprised by my kindness, gave me a very grateful look, and said, "Yes."

He told me he had often felt insignificant. It was rare for him to have older man who he respected take an interest in him. I told him, "God is a loving Father who is taking an interest in you right now. He loves you and wants you to be His son." I explained the Gospel to him in simple language and asked him if he had ever made the decision to receive the Lord. He said, "No sir, I haven't, because no one has ever explained it to me before like you just did." After asking him if he wanted to receive the Lord right now, he agreed.

I told him I could lead him in a prayer to receive the Lord. It was mid-morning, and he was sitting across the table from me in the empty dining room. We reached out to touch hands as we prayed. As I led him in a simple prayer to receive the Lord, the Holy Spirit's presence was tangible in the room. I could feel a stream of his warm tears hitting the top of my hand as we prayed together. This was the best Christmas gift I (and he) could ever receive! A son's identity was changed that day as this young man received a revelation of God's love and grace.

## Redefining Your Identity

I'm a guy who likes to teach on identity. My identity teaching began with God revealing to me how much He enjoys me as a son. This revelation transformed me on a personal level. God basically redefined my identity. Knowing that I became the boy who brings him joy was not something I experienced in my childhood. And still today, God is taking the identity revelation and expanding it beyond myself. When God reveals something to us, He has the ability to expand it, changing the identity of people, families and nations.

It's bigger than us; He doesn't stop at just changing your identity when He gives you a new nature. He's able to change the identity of His whole redeemed family, which is called the church, and make it as healthy as the Godhead. He can redefine the identity of a family, and then He's able to take the church and call it a nation. The church is called a nation in 1 Peter. When Jesus died and was crucified, He actually formed a new nation! Part of the benefit of His atoning work is that all people groups now get included in Christ, and God formed an entirely new identity for the church: a nation.

I want to talk about God's epic ability to reveal Himself. First, He reveals Himself through people (individuals), then through families, and then by His, holy nation, the church.

You may be familiar with Habakkuk 2:14, *"For the earth will be filled with the knowledge of the glory of the Lord as the waters, cover the sea."* This verse made me wonder this: what is the average depth of the oceans in the world? I decided to look it up. If you take the average depth of every ocean, it's 11,000 feet. I did some calculations, and that is two miles. So, the average depth of the world's oceans are two miles deep. When this verse hints at the amount of water covering the sea, this is bigger than just a rainstorm! The Lord is promising that He will saturate the earth to a level of two miles deep with a knowledge of His glory.

I believe we can define God's glory as His goodness. In Exodus 33, we read of Moses and God speaking to each other. Moses said, *"Show me your glory."* And God says, *"I will cause my goodness to pass over you,"* and so God's glory is equivalent to His goodness. John 1:14 reads, *"...and the word became flesh and lived among us and we beheld, his glory, even as the only begotten, Son of God, truly unique one of a kind."*

In beholding the glory of Jesus, I want you to know that Jesus is the most accurate revelation of God to man. You can't get a more accurate picture than that. And God has revealed Himself to us through prophecy and through history. But the most accurate revelation of God is Jesus Himself.

During His earthly ministry, mankind beheld His glory. But if glory means goodness, then Jesus is the unmitigated expression of God's goodness to mankind. And He is unique; When it comes to His glory, He has no rival. We sing about that, don't we? He has no rival in His glory, which means His ability to demonstrate His goodness and include everyone has no equal.

But God is not stopping with revealing His goodness *to* us. He has the power to transform us so He is able to reveal His goodness *through* us. And that is incredibly exciting, isn't it? It's exciting to be radically transformed by God's love. If His love changes your personal identity, your view of yourself, then that equips you to become part of God's healthy, redeemed family. When you are an unhealthy son, you will not be part of a healthy family Kingdom or a redeemed family at church. Why is this? Because you will always be competing with the other people, thinking the Father doesn't have enough love, provision or success to go around.

But when you discover that you are loved for who you are rather than for what you do, then there's no competition necessary. The transformed identity of a son or daughter will lead to church becoming healthy family, which is exactly what Jesus prayed for in John 17.

God becomes a man, so that we might become the sons of God. He becomes like us so we could become like Him. He takes on our nature so we can take on His nature. If any man be in Christ, he is a whole new creation.

The Incarnation, that is Jesus becoming a baby, becoming a man, was necessary to accomplish the atoning work. But Incarnation is also the pattern by which He transforms people groups, families and nations. That means God is progressively expanding the expression of Himself.

I feel this sense about God's heart: He's got a lot of confidence. God does not even have a hint of insecurity about creating mankind with free will. He was not worried about us rejecting Him! He was fully confident that that He could win our hearts if we got to know Him. And so, He is also fully confident that He can cover the earth to two miles deep with a knowledge of His glory. And did you know? He has a strategy to do just that. His strategy is to transform the identity of people, then families, and then His holy nation.

I feel the confidence of God in this, like He has given me a glimpse of His strategic power to transform. And the way He transforms is He transforms things to become an expression of Himself. Isn't that amazing? So, a redeemed son takes on the identity of his Father.

In the book of Romans, we read that all creation is groaning for three things. First, it is to see the manifestation of the mature sons of God. Creation longs to see these redeemed sons taking on the identity of their Father. Second, all creation is groaning for the redeemed family of God to take on the identity of the Godhead in humility and unity, expressing healthy family. Third, all of creation is groaning for a holy nation, the church, to rise up in the earth with its arms around the world, inviting every people group into the family of God.

This is the comprehensive purpose in the earth, and there is no doubt God has the power to accomplish it. Don't you like the fact that God is pretty confident in His ability? I like it. This is God's power to change the identity of people, families and nations.

As we look at Romans chapter 8, we read that God did not give us the spirit of religious duty. Aren't you glad? You have been set free from the religious performance treadmill. God loves you, not for what you do, but for who you are. God doesn't just have love;

He *is* love. So that means He has decided to love us, and He will not change His mind.

I am so grateful to be off all forms of perfectionism and being driven by performance. Earning affection is not necessary in God's Kingdom, and that goes on to say, you didn't receive the spirit of religious duty, leading you back into the fear of never being good enough.

Have you ever felt the torment of not being good enough? I think this is common among humans. The Lord has an antidote for that. He says you've received the *spirit of full acceptance* or the *spirit of adoption*.

In folding you into the family of God, you will never have to feel like an orphan. As He rises up within you, your spirit will join Him saying the words of tender affection, "Beloved Father." I love the title of Holy Spirit in this Romans 8 passage – the spirit of full acceptance, or in King James, the spirit of adoption. This has a powerful meaning. It is the Holy Spirit's job to reveal to you how much affection the Father has for you.

God loves you for who you are, not for what you do, and He doesn't stop loving you if you do bad things. He is not inspired to love you if you do good things, either. He has decided to love you, and He's not changing his mind. He is a big-hearted Father who knows we can be slow learners. For some reason, humanity is very slow at learning that the Father feels affection for us. He has deployed the spirit of adoption to convince us, by repetition, about the Father's affection for us.

In Matthew 3:16, we read that the Father spoke from Heaven at Jesus' baptism and said, *"This is my beloved Son in whom. I'm well pleased,"* I'd like to rephrase that to say, "This is the boy who brings me joy!"

Look at this amazing truth in Romans 8:16: *"For the holy spirit makes God's fatherhood real to us as he whispers to our innermost being you are God's beloved child."* It's the Holy Spirit's job to help you discover the reality of your sonship.

And so, you have the right to believe, according to the Bible, that God loves you just as much as He loves Jesus. That means, you could accurately say, "I'm the boy who brings Him joy," or "I'm the girl who makes Him twirl!"

Jesus loves us, just as the Father has loved Him (John 17:23). That means you are not a second-class son or daughter in the Kingdom of God. That means that the intensity of the Father's love for us is equal to the intensity of the Father's love for Jesus.

A redeemed son gets redefined because of the Father's love for him. All redeemed sons have a new nature, but that nature is forged through the lens of the Father's love for us. This is super good news. That means your former identity, your "bad" self, your old nature has been forever buried. The Bible says that in your water baptism, Jesus included Himself. He included you in Himself, and then He buried your sin nature forever and left it in the ground. He deprived your old nature of its ability to stay alive.

Sometimes in religious circles, we try to reanimate our old man nature, and then improve it. I'm telling you, that is wasted effort. The enemy tries to get us to do what God has already done for us. He tries to get the believer employed in wasted effort. But the truth is, you can't kill yourself. You can't bring to death your old nature, because the Lord has done that for you. He included you in Himself and left your old nature buried in the ground. Then, when He rose from the dead, He also included you in Himself, which means you have risen with Him and are a new creature in Christ. You are no longer tethered to your old nature. In rising with Him you defy the downward gravitational pull of your old nature.

Imagine this: at the moment of His resurrection, He's rising, leaving earth's surface. He is including you in Himself as He defies gravity – the gravitational pull of your old nature. He's showing there is victory; your new nature in Him overcomes the downward gravitational pull of your old nature. The new nature wins because you go up with Him. You ascend, you don't get pulled down. So, then He severs the tether that keeps you linked to the identity of your old nature, and you go up with Him like a helium balloon. Can you picture it?

Because He's proven the power of your new nature defying the gravity of the old nature, that means our new nature is now our true identity! That is great news! I've said this before, but I want you to deeply understand this. The revelation of this truth has changed the way I deal with myself when I am not walking in my true nature. For example, on occasion, I may get annoyed by my wife and raise my voice to her. Now, the Holy Spirit convicts me of sin like this and does not let me get away with it. So, when I feel convicted, I repent (change my mind to line up in agreement with God). When I repent, I change the wording of *how* I repent, so that I'm not groveling or beating myself up.

Here's how I do it: "Forgive me, Lord, for expressing my old nature." And then I ask Him, "Will you coach me and help me to express my true nature?" My failure in my behavior does not redefine my identity. I am continually a loved and accepted son of God.

## A Redeemed Family

A redeemed family takes on the identity of the Godhead in their expression of healthy family. I want you to see how this is systematic and progressive. This is God's plan to cover the earth with His glory, because He has the power and opportunity to express

Himself. Through yielded individuals, He changes their identity. Then, through His redeemed family, He changes the whole way the family operates, making it a perfect reflection of the health of the Godhead.

Remember, the Godhead is the template. The Godhead is the prototype family in the earth that existed before humans. And that family, the Godhead, is the pattern by which God gives grace to the church to become just like them as we see in the prayer in John 17:21: *"I pray that they may all be one as you father are in me and I in you that they may be one in us that the world may know that you sent me."* Focus on the last phrase of that passage: *"...so that the world may know that you sent me."* What a powerful statement that is. Jesus is staking all His credibility on whether we get it right.

If I were Jesus, I would have not prayed that. I would have said something like, "When the world discovers who I am, then they will know that You sent me," but He doesn't say that. He's got more confidence in you than you can imagine. He has more confidence in us. He has issued the church grace to become as healthy as the Godhead! Jesus put all His eggs in the church basket. He's going to stake all His credibility as to whether He was sent from the Father on whether we display the true nature of His church: a healthy family.

And the dynamic of the relationship between Jesus and His Father is a whole lot of mutual joy, mutual love and delight. Their relationship is the healthiest that has ever existed, and that is the pattern we are empowered and given grace to function in.

## A Holy Nation

When we think about His progression – person, family, nation – let's discuss the last one: God's progressive expression of Himself

112

in a holy nation. His holy nation is meant to wrap its arms around the world and invite every people group into the family of God. The church is defined as a nation.

In 1 Peter chapter 2, it says, *"But you are a chosen people, a royal priesthood, a holy nation, God's special possession that you may declare the praises of him who called you out of darkness into his wonderful light."*

Notice how God is crafting in His redemption. He crafted a redefined individual and called them a son. He crafted a redefined family to demonstrate the health of the Godhead. Then, He crafts a whole new nation composed of redeemed families across the world.

God is a big-hearted Father who is inviting every people group into Himself. Literally no people group anywhere is excluded from becoming part of God's new nation. God is the most inclusive being in the universe.

God's redeemed family, from every ethnos or people group, has now become healthy enough to be integrated together into a holy nation. He designed the progressive nature of this: God transforms people, then He transforms families, then He integrates families together across the earth of every nation and people group, and then He takes his new nation and wraps His arm around the whole world, inviting them into family.

This is how He's going to cover the earth with the knowledge of His glory. He is unlimited in His ability to transform people, families and nations, and then make them an expression of Himself.

I feel confident about this. God is 100% competent and does not make promises like this on a whim. "I will cover the earth with a knowledge of My glory," is a big promise. And to a level equivalent to two miles deep. He does not make promises without having a strategic plan to fulfill His promise. Let me show you His plan, and it should make you happy.

God made an irrevocable vow to Moses: *"'As surely as I live,' saith the Lord, 'the knowledge of my glory will cover the Earth, even as the waters, cover the sea.'"* Then, in Isaiah 9:6 we are promised, *"Of the increase of his government and of his peace, there shall be no end."*

Aren't you glad you are part of a holy nation called to be as inclusive with God's love as God Himself is?

In Ephesians 2:15, we read that our reconciling piece is Jesus. He has made Jew and non-Jew one in Christ by dying as our sacrifice. *"Ethnic hatred has been dissolved by the crucifixion of his precious body on the cross. The legal code that stood condemning every one of us has now been repealed by his command. His triune essence has made peace between us by starting over—forming one new race of humanity, Jews and non-Jews fused together in himself!"* (TPT)

Christ Jesus has broken down every wall of prejudice that separated us. And now, He has made us equal through our union with Christ. Every attempt in the earth to try to bring unity between people groups is wasted effort if we don't understand Ephesians 2:15, because God has already done it. God has already dissolved ethnic hatred by His cross.

He has already taken every nation and every ethnic group and considered them equal; He includes them in Himself and redefined humanity. Again, the enemy tries to get the church to do something that God has already done for them.

I care about the grief and the injustice of various people groups in America and throughout the nations of the earth. I care about that, and I have empathy for it. But if we do not get this revelation, then we'll be trying to do something in our own ability that God has already done on the cross. As the church, we need to awake to the fact that God has already done it and start to live that way.

Through Christ, ethnic hatred has been dissolved. It also says the legal code that stood condemning every one of us has now been repealed by His command. His Triune essence has made peace with us by starting over *forming one new race of humanity.*

He redefined the identity of the whole world. He formed a whole new race. And God's new nation is inclusive rather than divisive. Jews and non-Jews are fused together in Himself. This is why inclusion and unity is effective, because we're not trying to do it by ourselves. The power of unity is that He included us in Himself, and He has the power to do it.

In Ephesians chapter 2, we see how the atoning work of God wrapped His arms around every people group, including them in Himself. We see Him forming one new man, or one new nation, in His image, in which all ethnic hatred is dissolved. This is everyone: suffering people groups like homeless, orphans, widows and the poor. He includes every suffering subgroup of humanity in Himself.

What grieves me man's tendency to decide who's more important, who's more valuable and who's less valuable, right? Across all cultures, societies and all people groups, we have the ability to form governmental segments, affluent segments or ethnic segments. We have a way to exclude people and create a value system that puts some people on the bottom.

Yet, in the Gospels, Jesus does exactly the opposite of this. We should be inspired by teachings that reveal His inclusivity. There are no people groups that are disqualified or excluded from God or from experiencing God's goodness.

In the Gospels, we see Jesus crossing society's lines. A leper, in Jewish culture or in religious culture, was considered unclean. But that does not keep the Lord from touching and healing a leper with His love. This now means everyone who is unclean according to the law is no longer disqualified from God's love!

Jesus was sent to the Jews, but He took time to minister to a Samaritan woman sitting at a well. This woman who'd had five husbands and was living with her current boyfriend was no longer disqualified from experiencing God's goodness! He crossed gender, religious and ethnicity lines with this encounter.

Jesus was also willing to go to a demonized heathen who was considered the lowest in the Hebrew value system. This is the lowest form of a human to a Hebrew's religious system: a demonized Gentile. And Jesus went out of His way, crossing the Sea of Galilee, to deliver the demonized Gentile, because again, no people group, no ethnic group, no bad-behaving person is disqualified from experiencing the love of God!

Remember, John chapter 1 says we beheld His (Jesus') glory. Man saw Him. We beheld His glory. We saw firsthand the mitigated glory of the expression of God's goodness. He allowed us to see Him, which means no one is disqualified. No one is excluded.

## An Upgrade

The church is now receiving an upgrade in how we view evangelism. We are not to view evangelism anymore as merely the Gospel of salvation. Our job is not just to get people saved. Although I want you to be equipped to lead people to the Lord, our real job is to be ambassadors of the outrageous goodness of God to every people group. We should have the same view that Jesus does: no one is excluded. We're going to purposely, intentionally navigate through every religious and societal barrier that devalues humans. When doing so, we will reach the most broken. The church is called to be an evangelist just like Jesus, which means no one is disqualified. We are valuing people who are different from us, and learning to deeply honor people who are different from us is the most fun thing ever.

I have been around the world on mission trips. When I do mission trips, I ask God to let me see something in each people group that I can honor. I don't come in as the American thinking, "I do everything better than them." No, I ask, "God, will You help me fall in love with this different people group?" He's always faithful to show me something they do well.

Then, I'm not flattering them, but God will open my eyes to see the value of someone different from me when I'm with them. When I have value for another people group, my ministry is empowered. It's not just a method; this is how we learn to love people who are different from us. I'm inspired to see the church rise up and become massively more effective at navigating through every barrier that keeps people from experiencing God's goodness.

**The Pattern**

Here is the end result of the Lord's atoning work:

- God revealed Himself to us in Christ.

- Then, He reveals Himself to us in a way that transforms us as individuals, then families, and then nations.

- Next, His holy nation (His church) navigates through every cultural and religious barrier that devalues people. The way the church operates surprises and blows people away with the unconditional goodness of God.

This is this is my way of defining evangelism. It's the goodness of God that will attract people to the transformation God wants for them. We don't require the transformation first. We show them the goodness of God *first*.

In the Gospels, this is exactly the way Jesus did it. He did not go up to badly behaving, hurting people and demand that they repent first. No, He just poured out His goodness for them to experience. He decided that no one was excluded, and then he transformed one life at a time.

John chapter 4's Samaritan woman was behaving badly, but He transforms her in such a way that she changes her whole city. Does she somehow deserve an experience with God's goodness? No, but this is who Jesus is.

## An Upgrade Prayer for You

It's my great joy to announce to the church that you will have an upgrade in evangelism. I release, in Jesus', name grace to be ambassadors of God's outrageous goodness to every people group that was previously disqualified. God, fill us now with Your Holy Spirit and Your love so that the groaning earth sees the manifestation of the sons of God in all the fullness of who we are in Christ Jesus.

We dedicate and consecrate ourselves as a people who will discover the outrageous goodness of God, and we will be ambassadors of Your outrageous goodness. We say yes to the mandate to purposely and intentionally navigate through every barrier that keeps people from experiencing Your goodness. Amen.

# ABOUT THE AUTHOR

For the past 37 years, Bill Burkhardt and his wife Sandy have been married and serving together in teaching and pastoral ministry and missions.

Bill came to Christ while in college, and his hunger for God's Word and presence increased. Bill started studying Christian doctrine and other Bible college subjects before finishing college.

Bill graduated from Virginia Tech with his Bachelor and Master's degree in science. After moving to San Diego, he continued to Bible school and began his life-long ministry journey.

Bill and Sandy's call is to come alongside pastors and believers to bring everyone into a higher level of encounter with God's love and freedom and to share the Father's heart with the rest of the world. In 2017, Bill and Sandy merged their church with Beach Chapel where they now serve as Associate Pastors.

Bill and Sandy have two amazing children: their son Tim and his wife Minah, and their daughter Betsy and her husband David, and two of the most incredible grandchildren God has ever created!

Connect more with Bill at www.fathers-heart-ministry.com